# HEAVEN
# IS
# HIGHERING

**THIRD EDITION**

# HEAVEN IS HIGHERING

## How To Obtain Spiritual Employment

*Weldon R. Johnson*

authorHOUSE®

*AuthorHouse™*
*1663 Liberty Drive*
*Bloomington, IN 47403*
*www.authorhouse.com*
*Phone: 833-262-8899*

*Published by AuthorHouse  05/10/2021*

*ISBN: 978-1-6655-1879-6 (sc)*
*ISBN: 978-1-6655-1877-2 (hc)*
*ISBN: 978-1-6655-1878-9 (e)*

*Library of Congress Control Number: 2021904575*

*Print information available on the last page.*

In memory of the angelic Ashlee T. Madison.
Ashlee served on earth as God's employee.
She received God's heavenly retirement when her
spirit was elevated on April 17, 2010.

# ❧ Acknowledgments ❧

All thanks and glory to Yahweh (Yah) and His Son, Yahshua Hamashiach—Christ the Messiah!

Special thanks to the family of Ashlee T. Madison. May she rest in peace.

I would like to express my sincere gratitude to my family: my darling wife, Victoria Johnson, for her love and encouragement in all that I do, and for her self-sacrifice and diligence as my research assistant, proofreader, and managing editor; my dad, Pastor Keneith Shepherd, and family; Mother Greta Stewart; my father-in-law, Vennie Livingston, Sr.; my mother-in-law, Betty Livingston; my sisters, Stephanie and Kenelle; my brothers, Ronnie Gray and Pastor Craig Frazier; my son, Jordan Christopher; my daughter, Sara Victoria; my niece, Olivia; my nephew, Kenny; my Uncle Hugh and Aunt Pam Jackson; and my overseers, Pastor Frank and Beverly Mclean, and the 5 a.m. prayer line family.

Special thanks to our friend, Dr. Angela M. Ball, for joining our team to assist with editing the first edition of my book.

Finally, I would like to extend a heartfelt thanks to Joyce and Jay at PostNet for teaming up with my wife and me to format this book and design the cover, as well as thank the staff at AuthorHouse Publishing Company for helping us proclaim this message all over the world!

# Contents

# Preface

God knew that I would step out in faith and do what He told me to do early one morning on March 29, 2010, at 6:39 a.m. On this blessed day, spring was just beginning when I unexpectedly heard His voice gently say, "Write a book. Write a book. Write a book."

Although I had previously given my life to God when He called upon me to write this book, I had never accomplished anything close to writing a book in my life! Besides, I didn't have the slightest clue where to begin. But what I did know was that when God tells you to do something, you should readily obey and completely trust Him. By writing a book that God, my Father, had inspired me to birth—I knew that my obedience to Him would create a wonderful opportunity for the lost people of the world to learn and develop an intimate relationship with Him, as well as revive the faith, hope, and love of believers who are seeking a deeper understanding of His purpose for their lives.

Writing this book is one of the most humbling yet notable works of art and blessings that He has ever given me the honor of achieving in my entire life! Who could have known what God was preparing me for except Him? This experience has helped me realize how vitally important it is for each of us to be still and listen to His voice when He talks to us and not say, "It's all in my head" (that is, doubting God is speaking).

God is saying more to you than you will ever know while here on earth. His relationship with you begins in your spiritual heart or mind. To the Creator of humankind, the life that He has given you and me is so precious in His sight. Sadly, most of us cannot comprehend the value God places on us through His unconditional love; thus, we take life for granted. The fact that He breathed life into the nostrils of man to make him a "living soul" is sufficient evidence that God has a divine purpose for our lives here on earth.

Some of the simple things in life that we take for granted, which He created for us to enjoy, are the clean air that we breathe, until we have polluted it; the clouds that accumulate and produce raindrops and rainbows to cool, nurture, calm, and remind us of His promise on earth; the breeze to cool and refresh us on a hot summer day; or the relaxing sounds of a rumbling thunderstorm on the first day of spring.

And oh, how refreshing are the five senses that He has so graciously bestowed upon us; they are simply amazing! In my opinion, His gifts of taste, touch, smell, sight, and sound are at the top of my list for what I enjoy the most in my earthly body. For without some or all these wonderful gifts, how would life be for us? I can't imagine what life would be like if our most generous Creator never provided us with some or all these gifts so that we are able to fully enjoy our lives on this side of heaven.

In Genesis 1, we find that when the Founder was making the blueprint for the construction of the earth, it only took Him six days to complete His work; and on the seventh day, He rested from His creation. Now, for earthly humans to comprehend this, it would take a stretch of the imagination to think that this planet called Earth (as magnificent as it is) only took six days for our Father to create. In our earthly minds, this is inconceivable. "For with God, *nothing* will be impossible!" (Luke 1:37 NKJV; emphasis added).

*His* power of thought, compared to ours, cannot be understood with our earthly (carnal) minds. However, it is possible to discern God's thoughts by using your spiritual conscience. For this reason, the Founder wants to higher (elevate) all His creation so that they would take on the same mindset as His and would be capable of doing the same things that He does by faith in Him. For all who appreciate the Founder's ingenuity and ability to actually speak things into existence, we stand in awe of the sheer magnitude of His presence, power, and authority!

As you read this book, which I wrote just for you, I encourage you to allow God to speak directly to your spiritual heart or mind, as He has shared His intimate message with me—*heaven is highering.*

Weldon R. Johnson

# Chapter 1

## On Earth as It Is in Heaven

This account starts in the beginning with the one who created *all* things in *heaven* and on *earth*—God, who is referred to in this story as the *Founder* or *the Boss* (read Genesis 1:1). Before time ever existed, God was here (read John 1:1). God, who is Alpha and Omega, is the beginning and the end of all things created (read Revelation 22:13). God is the *only* true God; the others are false gods whom the heathens' worship (read Deuteronomy 4:35, 39, 6:4; Psalm 86:10; Isaiah 43:10–13; Matthew 4:10; Mark 12:29).

God is made up of three bodies or persons all wrapped up into Himself. He is *One* God who is in three persons, known as the *Godhead* or *Trinity of persons*, which, according to 1 John 5:1–12 and 20, consists of

- the *Father* (God in the Spirit),
- the *Son* (Jesus Christ, the second person of the Trinity), and
- the *Holy Spirit* (the third person of the Trinity).

There are three separate and distinctly divine functions of the Godhead. The function of the Father is to choose whom He will save (Ephesians 1:4–6). The Son's assignment is to heal, deliver, and redeem lost sinners to the Father (Ephesians 1:7). And the Holy Spirit's assignment is to seal the relationship between God and humankind (Ephesians 1:13). These three persons or bodies of the Godhead are in complete union with one another regarding all matters in heaven and on earth. They do nothing apart from one another. Let me further explain this relationship through the eyes of our earthly system of government.

*God* is a title much like the word *government*. A government has many branches and functions, but it is called by one name. For instance, the three branches of government are the city, state, and federal branches. Also, the foundation on which our government firmly stands includes the executive, legislative, and judicial branches. Each branch operates in separate arenas and is uniquely powerful. With that power, each branch checks the other to ensure accountability in order to protect the best interest of the people, not the government itself. In other words, they work together for the common good of the whole.

In comparison to the three branches of government, God the Father is a Spirit and is the Founder or Creator and Boss of everything, as well as the Author of the Handbook (Bible or Word of God) that governs everyone in the whole universe. Jesus, the Son of God, in His divine nature, is truly God or the Eternal Word. In modern-day language, Jesus is considered the Bible in "living color."

With His human nature, which He took from His mother (Mary), He is positively man. He came to earth as the chief executive officer (or CEO) to show us how to preside over earthly matters and seek and save sinful men or women. The Holy Spirit is also divine in nature and is considered the general manager (or GM), who presides directly over (or inside) the hearts and minds of the Founder's employees to enable them to carry out His righteous will. Like the government, the Godhead works together for the common good of true believers in Christ—the employees of the Founder.

Additionally, the Godhead is much like water, which has three different forms based on the environment. In above-freezing temperatures, water remains in its liquid form. In below-freezing temperatures, water converts into ice, which is its solid form. When heated, water converts into a vapor, which is its gas form. But it's still water.

In comparison to water, human beings are made up of mind, body, and spirit. The physical part of us is the body and the mental part of us is our mind, will, and intellect—the psyche. Both the mind and body are temporary and are perishing daily; however, the spirit, which is really who we are inside, is eternal and will live forever.

In our human state, about 60 percent of our body is made up of physical water, the brain (mind) is composed of 70 percent water, and about 83 percent of our blood is water. Consequently, we need clean water to live and to use for practically everything, such as cooking, bathing, cleaning, and maintaining a healthy body, as well as for participating in many activities involving water. But our spirit does not need physical water for survival; it needs supernatural food.

---

**Both the mind and body are temporary and are perishing daily; however, the Spirit, which is really who we are inside, is eternal and will live forever.**

---

Just as we need physical water to maintain the life of our physical bodies, we need the Spirit of God (Jesus)—who is called the Living Water—in order to connect with Him. It is the Spirit of God living in a person, not the natural mind or body, that makes him or her come alive. This is because the body without the Spirit of God is dead, which is why unbelievers cannot operate in the realm of faith. These statements can be verified in James 2:26 (NKJV), which states, "For as the body [physical and mental] without the Spirit is dead, so faith without works is dead also" (emphasis added).

Then Genesis 2:7 (KJV) states,

> And the Lord God formed man of the dust of the ground, and breathed into his nostrils the breath of life; and man became a living soul.

> **It is the Spirit of God living in a person, not the natural mind or body, that makes him or her "come alive."**

These scriptures prove three things, but we're only going to focus on two points to stick to the subject matter. (Faith will be discussed in another chapter later in this book.) First, they prove that God created man (from the dust of the ground), and He blew His Spirit into man's nostrils, then man became a living soul. The main point here is that man was not alive until God breathed His Spirit into him. Every breath that you and I take comes from God. We cannot 'live, move, or have our being' without possessing His Spirit inside of us. The second point that these scriptures prove is that without the Spirit of God breathed into man, man would have remained a corpse. Your body, without the indwelling of God's Spirit, is dead.

As a matter of fact, you can be physically alive and walking around, but if you haven't invited Jesus into your life, you are spiritually dead. I am sure you have seen the walking dead among your family, friends, colleagues, professional affiliations, and even in your church. And yet, many of these people don't even know they're spiritually dead until someone delivers an insightful message that inspires, awakens, liberates, and transforms their life from indulging in dead works to receiving Jesus Christ as their personal Savior. Without God's Spirit, you possess a carnal (ungodly) mind and fleshly body, which means you cannot think, speak, or behave Christlike. Therefore, your mind and body without God's Spirit is dead! Only the message of Jesus Christ can captivate and transform your thinking, influence your ideas, shape your character, and increase your wisdom so that the Spirit of God will come alive and take residence in you. So throughout your life, it is vitally important that you continue to nurture your relationship with God so that you will continue to be spiritually alive and experience His peaceful presence.

You've heard the cliché: No God, no peace. Know God, know peace. In our natural state of mind or fleshly mind, we are prone to follow lustful desires of the flesh, the world, and Satan—which lead to sin, division in relationships, mental confusion, and eternal death in hell (when our physical body dies). In our spiritual state of mind, on the other hand, we follow godly principles, which lead to righteousness, peace of mind, healthy relationships, and eternal life in heaven (when our physical body dies). Only believers of Jesus can be spiritually alive because they have an intimate relationship with Him, which helps them think, speak, and behave righteously (1 Corinthians 2:10–11). Nonbelievers who indulge in the flesh and all its lusts are spiritually dead even though they are walking around in their bodies. A carnally and spiritually-minded person may experience similar problems in life, but the spiritually-minded person will go through them with peace, while the carnally minded person will be overwhelmed with tormenting fear, anxiety, doubt, and worry. This explains why Jesus said in John 4:14 (KJV; emphasis added),

> But whosoever drinketh of the water that I shall give him shall never thirst: but the water that I shall give him shall be in him a well of water springing up into *everlasting* life.

And then Jesus assured us in John 6:35 (KJV):

> And Jesus said unto them, "I am the bread of life: he that cometh to Me shall never hunger; and he that believeth on Me shall never thirst."

Jesus, the CEO, is the Living Water that we need daily for our healing, deliverance, redemption, and victorious living. Following Him will lead our spiritual mind to abundant living while we're here on earth and will lead our spiritual bodies into heaven upon the end of our physical life.

Understanding God in three persons will give you, the reader, a deeper awareness of and appreciation for His diversity of power in all forms of His creation. The creation of God's corporation will be discussed in greater detail in the next chapter. For now, we shall explore the beginning of heaven and earth and how words, especially the Word of God, create your circumstances in life. In John 1:1–3 (NIV), it is recorded accordingly:

> In the beginning was the Word, and the Word [Jesus or the living Bible] was with God, and the Word was God. He [Jesus and the

Holy Spirit] was in the beginning with God [the Father]. All things were made through Him, and without Him nothing was made that was made.

Then in John 1:14 (NIV), it is written,

And the Word became flesh [Jesus] and dwelt among us [on earth], and we beheld His glory, the glory as of the only begotten of the Father [God], full of grace and truth.

In these scriptures, we come to realize how powerful and extraordinary the very Word of God is—in heaven and on earth. Jesus was with God when the worlds (plural) were formed, and He later came to earth to fulfill (in Scripture) all that God said was going to happen. Although Jesus had a short life here on earth, He did fulfill His purpose before ascending back to heaven. Additionally, in Matthew 24:35 (KJV), God declared (emphasis added),

Heaven and earth will pass away, but the Word of God will *last* forever!

This scripture validates that the Word of God is active and alive forever! Scripture wasn't written by men of superior intellect. Instead, they were written by men who were inspired by God through the Holy Spirit (read 1 Corinthians 2:10). And because the Handbook was inspired by God, that means you can totally put your faith in it, pattern your life after it, and bet your future on it. The secular world will defame, scorn, disregard, and even pervert the Handbook. They will try to destroy it, ban it, or twist its trustworthiness. But make no mistake about it, God or His Word can never be destroyed! The Founder is the King eternal, immortal, and invisible God! His Word lives forever! Peter, one of Jesus's beloved disciples, referred to the Handbook as "the incorruptible and indestructible, living" Word of God—meaning that it is full of life, and even the gates of hell can't prevail against it!

According to Hebrews 4:12 (NIV; emphasis added),

The Word of God is living, and powerful, and sharper than *[any]* two-edged sword, piercing even to the dividing asunder of soul and spirit, and of the joints and marrow, and is a discerner of the thoughts and intents of the heart!

It is so alive and sharp that when spoken, the Word has the power to create your situation—either blessing or curse, success or failure, or life or death! (Read Deuteronomy 30:19–20.) No, the Bible is not the practice of black magic, witchcraft, psychic powers, or anything evil. Instead, it is full of God's promises for those who obey Him, and it also enlightens us about curses that come upon those who rebel against God's principles. That's why, as human beings, the words that proceed out of our mouth should always correspond with the scriptures in the Bible. What you say has the power to build up or tear down a person, marriage, organization, plan, idea, or thing. For this reason, you must be very careful how you use words toward others, as well as to yourself.

> **Because the Handbook was inspired by God, that
> means you can totally put your faith in it, pattern
> your life after it, and bet your future on it.**

Now that you know the power of words, especially the power of God's Word, you should honor and respect what He has to say about His plans for you, His creation. It was God the Father, the Son, and the Holy Spirit who established the origin of all things that were created in heaven and on earth. And it is His Spirit, the Living Water, that makes us come alive so that we will understand and live our lives according to His divine will. Now that you have a clear understanding about Him and His nature, along with the knowledge of His divine design, we will continue with His message to all—heaven is highering.

*Death and life are in the power of the tongue: and they that love it shall eat the fruit thereof.*

—Proverbs 18:21 (KJV)

# Chapter 2

## The Creation of God's Corporation

The characters in this historical message are based on the *Godhead*: God the Father, Son (Jesus), and Holy Spirit (the Third Person). Other characters, who will be discussed in this truthful account, include the heavenly hosts—spiritual beings called angels and the earthly beings called *humankind*, who are God's employees.

Each of these characters will have the same characteristics even though each exists in two different realms: heaven in relation to the spiritual realm and earth in relation to the physical realm. In both realms, God the Father, who in this message is referred to as the Founder or Boss, has established an order of laws, rules, policies, and functions that reflect His plans and desires for all that He has created in heaven and on earth.

Heaven, the corporate headquarters, and earth, the branch office, will be referred to as the company in which God—the Founder, Boss, and Owner—is the major stockholder, and Jesus is the CEO. The Holy

Spirit is the GM. The fallen angel is Satan (a.k.a., the devil), and his residence is in hell, or the lower level.

As with the development of an earthly corporation in which the Founder first creates the business plan that spells out the corporate location, its goals and objectives, its mission, its funding sources, its services or products, its departments, and its employees—God, the original Founder, developed the master plan for the whole world!

God's business plan is the plan of salvation. His business mission is in the human service industry. His main goal and objective is to save humankind from spiritual death, hell, and destruction. His funding source is endless. His departments are all nations, and His employees are angels and humankind.

The angels are employed at the corporate headquarters and branch office, and humankind is employed at the branch office (a.k.a., earth).

All that God has set in order ensures His company's integrity and assures that the company's foundation will endure for eternity. The order in which God established His company is similar to our modern-day government or kingdom. Heaven (a.k.a., the headquarters of God's company), is to be introduced to all humankind, the earthly employees. As a part of God's government or kingdom, He also appointed department heads, who are the kings and rulers (upper management) of nations.

In this modern day, the department heads (upper management) are regarded as our pastors, teachers, (true) prophets, evangelists, and apostles. All of whom are a part of the ministry of the gospel of Jesus Christ and have been given authority from God to oversee humankind and carry out the Founder's orders for three reasons: the perfecting of the saints (His employees), the work of the ministry, and the edifying (or learning) of the body of Christ (His educational institution, the church). This statement was established in Ephesians 4:11–13 (KJV) as the following:

> And He gave some, apostles; and some, prophets; and some, evangelists; and some, pastors and teachers; For the perfecting of the saints, for the work of the ministry, for the edifying of the body of Christ: Till we all come in the unity of the faith, and of the knowledge of the Son of God, unto a perfect man, unto the measure of the stature of the fullness of Christ.

By these scriptures, we come to understand that the Founder gave us spiritual overseers to bind us together as one body into the unity of the faith and give us knowledge of Christ the CEO so that we would become perfect and exemplify Christlike behavior. The similarities between God's company and our modern-day government system are quite impressive in the way that God employs both angels and humankind to do His good and perfect will. What would one expect from such a remarkable *Boss*?

God is the original inventor of all good things. His first inventions are a part of our basic necessities for life, such as light, darkness, the sun, the moon, the stars, rivers, oceans, aquatic life, birds, beasts, and creeping things (read Genesis 1). He created the four seasons—spring, summer, winter, and fall—for His purpose (read Genesis 1). Each season was perfectly designed to keep balance and harmony on the earth. For without the four seasons, the earth would be a dreadful place for life. When He created the heavens, He did not spare one single thought, "jot or tittle" on how the moon, stars, and galaxies would work together in perfect harmony. Just look up at the sky on a clear moonlit night, and you can't help but marvel at what God has done. In your amazement, you have to ask yourself, "How is this all possible without the assistance of a supernatural God?"

In the Bible, or the Handbook as it is referred to in this account, in Job 38:1–7, God rebukes one of His earthly employees, named Job, for questioning Him about things that were "too wonderful" for him to know. In Job 38:4 (KJV), God emphatically answered Job, saying,

> Where were you when I laid the foundations of the earth, formed the stars and created the heavens?

For that matter, where was Job when He created anything? He was nowhere because he had not yet existed.

In Job 42:1–3, it is observed that Job immediately changed his tune (from complaining and questioning God) by humbling himself to the knowledge and counsel of the Almighty to win His favor and be healed of his illness. By yielding to God's authority, we learn that Job's health was completely restored, and he was rewarded double for all the trouble he endured (Job 42:10–15)!

Sometimes when we, God's employees, are facing tremendous trials that produce anguish, anger, frustration, and even fear, we must be ever so careful not to approach God as if we know more than He does because it can lead us down the wrong path and have us questioning the sovereignty and will of an all-wise Boss. Since God is the potter and we are the clay, He knows exactly what circumstances we need to endure in order to mold, reshape, and transform us into the vessels that will bring the best benefit and most good in our lives, which will also bring the ultimate glory to His name. This statement can be confirmed in scripture in Jeremiah 18:4–6 (KJV):

> And the vessel that He made of clay was marred in the hand of the potter: so he made it again another vessel, as seemed good to the potter to make it. Then the word of the Lord came to me, saying, "O house of Israel, cannot I do with you as this potter?" saith the Lord. "Behold as clay is in the potter's hand, so are ye in mine hand, O house of Israel."

Knowing that God has the power to form our lives into something that will bring Him glory and honor, it is always better to sit in a quiet place and meditate on His Word to learn all that He designed for us, His employees.

We should be especially thankful that we have a more than competent Boss who considers all things when He plans to do something. His insight and foresight are flawless and perfect in every way. Because God is omniscient, He has the vision to see far into the corridors of time, which is an ability that we don't primarily possess. If we could understand all there is to know about God, including correctly predicting the future, then we would become equal to or greater than Him. Surely, He would never allow that to happen; God would never make Himself unnecessary in the lives of His own creation. He created us to depend solely on His wisdom for guidance in life. Thus, He saw fit to give us only partial knowledge of things to come through being in fellowship with Him. Evidence of these statements can be found in 1 Corinthians 13:9, 12 (KJV):

> For we know in part and we prophesy in part. For we see only through a glass, darkly; but then face to face: now I know in part; but then shall I know even as also I am known.

> **God would never make Himself unnecessary
> in the lives of His own creation.**

Even now, the Founder knew that His employee would write this story—to completely give Him all the glory! He knew this even though the author of this book has never written a book before nor succeeded in a high school English class. To my surprise, as well as yours, it only took me forty days to write this book; though I cannot say the same for my editors, who hold masters and PhD-level secular degrees.

They told me that this book had surpassed their regular graduate-level studies, which prompted them to humble themselves and constantly revisit the Scriptures and parables in the Bible because they had no prior professional experience editing books, especially Christian books. (Dr. Ball has a background in business, and my wife has degrees in psychology, special education, and real estate.) Thus, they had to seek *biblical* knowledge and wisdom from God to become more *spiritually* conscious to acquire an understanding to assist me with the completion of this book. The point that I want to make here is this: God appointed unto me unbiased editors who did not look down on me (based on my past failures in high school English class) before they could see the blessing that I could be to them and others in the world. (Because of the encouragement I received from Dr. Angela Ball and my wife, I decided to let go of the fear of failing English and enrolled back in school. Now I can honestly testify that I successfully completed my high school education with honors! Moreover, as a result of reading this book, Dr. Ball decided to receive Jesus the CEO as her personal Savior, and she is living a victorious life today!)

Once my editors read this book, they were convinced that formal or higher education alone cannot supersede God's wisdom. And it wasn't until I came into the full knowledge of God and His plan for my life that I overcame my past failures and pressed toward my higher calling. Even though I had managed to open a successful massage clinic at the tender age of nineteen and held a prestigious title as a massage therapist and instructor at a community college, I still wasn't emotionally whole until God became first place in my life.

This is because God can use your past hurts, disappointments, and failures to strengthen and elevate your life. Failure is not final if a lesson is gained, and progress is made. Nevertheless, this revelation is yet mind-boggling, even for the most astute among us, since it contradicts human logic. Let me explain why.

---

**God can use your past hurts, disappointments, and failures to strengthen and elevate your life.**

---

**Failure is not final if a lesson is gained, and progress is made.**

---

In the natural realm, we look for great résumés, achievements, and degrees to qualify a person for a specific career path or job assignment. But in the spiritual realm, God chooses His servants based on availability for learning and growing, not book knowledge or intellectual abilities alone. In other words, God qualifies the unqualified who readily make themselves available for His service.

For the highly educated and economically elite to see that God also raises up what they deem as common people to perform great and mighty works is truly perplexing to the minds of the ungodly (ugly), arrogant, and disbelieving. (I'm not saying that there aren't any Christians among the highly educated or economically elite, because they do exist in large numbers. However, higher education tends to make well-educated people feel as though they are bigger than, smarter than, and more qualified than those who are unlearned and untrained by the *world's system* of obtaining it.) But you will discover in 1 Corinthians 1:25–26 (KJV) this biblical truth (emphasis added):

> Because the foolishness of God is wiser than men; and the weakness of God is stronger than men. For ye see your calling [it's a calling, not a career], brethren, how that *not* many wise men [or truly godly men] pursue after the flesh [the things of this world], *not* many mighty, *not* many noble [or highly educated men], are called [by God]: But God hath chosen the foolish things of the world [those that are least likely to be chosen by men] to confound the wise; and God hath chosen

the weak things of the world [the formally uneducated, but godly] to confound the things which are mighty; And base [low and humble] things of the world, and things which are despised [true Christians], hath God chosen, yea, and things which are not (high-ranking), to bring to nought [nothing] things that are: That *no* flesh [man or woman] should glory in His presence.

> **God qualifies the unqualified who readily makes themselves available for His service.**

God does not qualify a person solely based on their ability, but on their availability. God will mightily bless and use anyone who will sincerely make himself or herself available for His employment regardless of their age, gender, race, ethnicity, religious affiliation, educational background, intellectual disability, or socioeconomic status! For example, in the book of Esther, God chose a poor, young, but wise orphan girl named Esther to become the queen of Persia to save her Jewish people, including herself, from being annihilated by Haman. She didn't have any parents to care for her, but her uncle Mordecai raised her to depend on God. As Esther humbled herself to follow the instructions of her uncle—which was to fast and pray for God's protection and favor to approach her husband's throne and discuss the matter surrounding her people—God granted her petition.

Rather than having Esther, Mordecai, and the Jews executed, Haman was hanged in the same gallows that he had prepared for them! And to top it all off, King Xerxes gave Mordecai the position that Haman once had in the kingdom! You will reap whatever you sow—good or bad. (You must read the book of Esther to gain a better understanding of Haman's jealousy toward Mordecai, which caused him to seek to kill all the Jews.)

You see, just because you're young (inexperienced), old (passed the age of opportunity), poor, male, female, black, Indian, or Hispanic doesn't mean that you lack wisdom or opportunity. The conditions in which Esther was born and raised didn't determine the awesome future that God had prepared for her; her availability to be used by Him did!

Like Esther, what matters most is that you align yourself with the purpose or calling that God has for your life, even if you don't look the part of greatness in the eyes of humankind.

People will say unkind and hurtful words to break your spirit. They will laugh and make jokes about your hardships, disabilities and unfair disadvantages; but as you make continuous efforts to do God's will, you will reach your divine destiny. Just don't ever give up! Even if you fail (and you will fail at something), never lose your enthusiasm. If you learn to fail with an enthusiastic attitude, you can quickly bounce back from any unfortunate situation. It boils down to having unity with God, daily seeking a personal relationship with Him, discerning His path for your life, and confidently stepping into it—that's what makes you an available instrument to be *mightily* used by Him! In Revelation 3:20 (KJV), Jesus says,

> Behold, I stand at the door, and knock: if any man hear my voice, and open the door, I will come in to him and eat with him, and he with me.

When you unify with Jesus, He will satisfy your desires to have an intimate relationship with Him as well as guide you along the *best* path for your life. You see, it's really not complicated at all. Either you're available or you're not.

While there are blessings to be received by those who would be available for the Founder's employment, at the same time, you must be aware that there are *haters* of the Founder as well. These beings are in opposition to the Founder's plans for humankind. They choose to believe what some *ex-employees* of the company have said rather than what the Boss has said in His original Handbook, the Bible. These haters make outrageous claims that totally contradict what our Founder has written in His Handbook.

There are even some ex-employees of the Founder who attribute their intelligence to their earthly degrees and their pompous social affiliations, which they have attained from earthly men. Such former employees often do not respect the Founder, or His company, as the One who made all this possible. You see, the Founder is not opposed to His creation obtaining earthly degrees and success as long as He is honored and glorified in *all* that they endeavor to do. Besides, He is the one who provides the abilities, resources, and opportunities for their success in life. In addition to this; God opens doors that no man can shut! Revelation 3:8 (NKJV), Jesus declares,

> I know your works. See, I have set before you an open door, and no one can shut it; for you have a little strength, and have kept My word, and have not denied My name.

Then in Psalm 68:19 (KJV), David exclaims,

> Blessed be the Lord, who daily loaded us with benefits, even the God of our Salvation.

Also, in Colossians 3:17 (ESV), it is written,

> And whatever you do, in word or deed, do everything in the name of the Lord Jesus, giving thanks to God the Father through Him.

These scriptures acknowledge the Founder as the source of everything that His creation possesses here on earth, including talents, skills, and resources. Therefore, you should always give credit to the Founder God as the source of *all* that He has done to favor and benefit you, whether or not you have accepted Him as your personal Savior. The reason why you should praise Him even if you have not yet committed your life to Him is because Psalm 150:6 (KJV) exclaims, "Let everything that hath breath praise the Lord!"

Even the small act of you simply waking up this morning deserves praise unto God because He didn't have to do it. But He decided to give you another chance to seek and find Him because He has a specific purpose for your life that may be different from what you're currently doing. According to Jeremiah 29:11-12 (GNT), God is saying to you, "I alone know the plans I have for you, plans to bring you prosperity and not disaster, plans to bring about the future you hope for. Then you will call on me. You will come and pray to me, and I will answer you. You will seek me, and you will find me because you will seek me with all your heart." You see, the Founder *always* has more in store for you than what your carnal mind could ever dream of. Your job is to seek Him wholeheartedly through prayer.

The haters of the Founder have always attempted to stop God's employees from praising and worshipping the Founder for all that He has or will do for His creation. These haters are employed by the one who is the original rebel (a.k.a., Satan, or the devil). In the parables, Satan is also referred to as the thief, the imposter, the tempter, the pretender, the enemy, the hater, and the outsider. He has multitudes of outcasts and disgruntled employees working for him. The mission of Satan is to steal, kill, and destroy all that the Founder created for good use by any means necessary—including *you*! John 10:10 (KJV) verifies this statement by announcing,

> The thief [Satan] comes not, but to steal, kill and destroy. But I [Jesus] came that they may have life, and have it more abundantly.

As you can gather from the above scripture, the Founder wants all humankind to have a "more abundant" life while here on earth, but the thief desires to steal, kill, and destroy you! According to Luke 22:31–32 (ESV), Jesus told Simon Peter, one of His beloved disciples, that Satan made this request to the Founder of the company:

> Simon, Simon, behold, Satan hath desired to have you, that he may "sift you as wheat": But I have prayed for thee, that thy faith fail not: and when thou art converted, strengthen thy brethren.

In the above scripture reference, the phrase *sift you as wheat* implies that Satan wanted to literally have permission from the Founder to devour or eat alive the flesh of Simon Peter, but God defeated Satan's plan—through *prayer*.

You see, Satan's employees are not difficult to identify. His employees speak, behave, and live *diametrically* opposed to the abundant life that the Founder mapped out for His creation in the Handbook. Satan's desire is to devour all humankind by first luring you to practice corruption so that he can abort the Founder's plans for your life here on earth. Once Satan aborts the plans that the Founder has for you, his ultimate desire is for your earthly life to be full of chaos, shame, guilt, doubt, fear, worry, and confusion and for your eternal life to end in hell. On the contrary, the Founder's desire is to give you a more abundant life so that you may fulfill His will for your life on earth then spend all eternity in heaven!

It is the job of these disgruntled employees to go into various departments (a.k.a., nations), within the earthly branch to disrupt and desensitize the atmosphere to have new or lost employees second-guessing all that the Founder has placed in the Handbook. The tactics used by this rebel clan—such as fear, doubt, threats, manipulation, lies, lust, and flattery of the tongue—make him very clever and gifted in doing evil works. But these evil deeds will have no power over you if you resist or reject them as soon as you recognize them and their enticing schemes. James 4:7 (NKJV) instructs us, "Therefore submit to God. Resist the devil and he will flee from you."

If you do not accept Satan's tactics and you resist him, then he will leave you alone! But if you invite him in, then you will become a partaker in evil doing. All it takes for Satan to wreak havoc in your life is for you to give him access by doing a "little" sin. Just think about it this way: Satan is you—without God. Whoever you obey is the person you love. You are either obeying (loving) God or obeying (loving) Satan; there is no such thing as straddling the fence.

If you use a little marijuana or a little cocaine, consume prescription pills to get high, have just one extramarital affair, or cheat on your taxes just "a little bit," then Satan is already working in your life. Furthermore, if you operate in hatred, anger, bitterness, malice, slander, gossip, greed, arguments, cursing, or speaking against others, then you are of your father—the devil.

---

**Satan is you—without God.**

---

When you prefer sin over righteousness, you're operating in the lust of the eyes, lust of the flesh, and the pride of life, which hurls you precisely in Satan's realm. By choosing to sin, you set yourself up to experience hell on earth; and if you don't correct your words, thoughts, and actions, then your eternal life is bound for hell! You see, when you disobey the Word of God, you make God have no effect in your life, which means that Satan is working in and through your life, to do His pleasure. The pleasures of sin today will lead to great penalties tomorrow.

---

**The pleasures of sin today will lead to great penalties tomorrow.**

---

God wishes no one to perish, but He allows everyone to choose the path they want to take. There are only two paths to choose from—the way that leads to righteousness (life) or the way that leads to sin (death). He said in Deuteronomy 30:9 (KJV),

> This day I call heaven and earth as witnesses against you that I have set before you life and death, blessings and curses. Now choose life, so that you and your children may live.

God wants to bless you with a good life on earth and hereafter! The way you live your life is ultimately your choice, but the consequences of your choices are ultimately in God's hands. No one but you can decide how you will live your life and where you want to end up eternally. That's why you should wisely consider His ways. According to 1 Corinthians 10:23, "All things are lawful for me, but not all things are helpful; all things are lawful for me, but not all things edify" (NKJV). Suffice it to say that some things you may desire are not good for you.

---

**The way you live your life is ultimately your choice, but the consequences of your choices are ultimately in God's hands.**

---

I know that what I am about to share with you will shock some of you who claim to love God but let me put a twist to this same issue by addressing the so-called believers. (You may not agree with me, but I am only telling you what the word says. Thus, the principles of God *never* change.)

Whoever says they love God but hate or will not help their own mother, father, sister, brother, or friend who is in need *is* a liar, and the truth is *not* in them. All they're doing is pretending with their words (just as Satan does) to love someone, but in their heart and in their actions, they hate them. In doing so, they profess that they're a Christian and that God is their Father, but deep inside their heart lies the root of hatred and deceit toward the person they say is their friend or loved one.

Therefore, they don't love God or the person they're pretending to love. Furthermore, they cannot possibly even *know* the true and living God! To know God requires living out His love by meeting the needs of family, brethren in Christ, and even enemies whenever a person has the resources to help. In this manner, one fulfills the instructions that Christ gave to His disciples. These statements can be confirmed by the following scriptural references found in 1 John 4:20 (KJV; emphasis added):

> If anyone says, "I love God," and hateth his brother, he is a liar: for he that loveth not his brother whom he hath seen, how can he love God whom he hath not seen?

Then, in 1 John 3:17 (KJV), it is written (emphasis added),

> Now, suppose a person has enough to live on and notices another believer in need. How can God's love be in that person if he does not help the other believer?

Also, in Romans 12:20 (NIV), it is written (emphasis added),

> If your enemy is *hungry*, feed him; if he is thirsty, give him something to drink. In doing this, you will heap burning coals on his head.

These scriptures are clearly understood. It is impossible to know God if you do not show love, compassion, and benevolence toward everyone, including your enemies. If you say you love God but refuse to obey these instructions in His Handbook, God says you are a liar and the truth is not in you! Therefore, if you are not employed by the Founder, performing good deeds with a loving and kind heart, then you are working for the thief, practicing corrupt deeds. This is clearly stated in Matthew 12:30 (KJV):

> Jesus said, "He that is not with Me is against Me; and he that gathered not with Me scattereth abroad."

Then, in John 8:44 (KJV), Jesus said to His opponents (emphasis added):

> Ye are of your father the devil [Satan], and the lusts of your father ye will do. He was a murderer from the beginning, and abode not in the truth, because there is no truth in him. When he speaketh a lie, he speaketh of his own: for he is a liar, and the father of it. And because I [Jesus] tell you the truth, ye believeth Me not.

The above scriptural references verify that anyone who is against the Founder God and His Son does not love or belong to them. Additionally, it implies that anytime a person is consumed with the deceptive lies of Satan, they become full of pride, fall prey to sin, and put themselves under Satan's authority.

In other words, if a person's inner disposition is not receptive to the Word of God, then he or she will reject the truth. Did you know that refusing to practice what you've learned about the Godhead is the same as rejecting the truth? When you reject the truth, you give into the lies of the devil who then becomes father over your life. You become spiritually diseased within your heart (mind) when you say that you love others with your mouth but refuse to show in your actions that you really do. In other words, the person who feeds with lies will not practice the truth, and the person of truth will not practice a lie.

---

**The person who feeds with lies will not practice the truth, and the person of truth will not practice a lie.**

---

An example of a person falling under the authority of Satan is found in Genesis 3:1–17. The Founder requested a first-fruit offering from Abel, who was a keeper of the sheep, and his brother, Cain, who was a tiller of the ground. By faith, Abel presented a blood offering to the Founder from one of his very best flock of sheep, and Cain presented an offering from the ground that he tilled from. However, Cain's was not the first-fruit offering that pleased the Founder. Since the Founder accepted Abel's offering (because he gave it by faith) but rejected Cain's offering (because he didn't give it by faith), the latter became jealously outraged, and without even thinking about the consequences of what he was about to do, he took matters into his own hands and murdered his brother.

This is an example of how Satan tempted Cain to question the Founder's judgment and authority in the matter and enticed him to covet his brother's reward to rebel against the commandments of the Founder (Thou shalt not kill, and thou shalt not covet). In other words, anytime a person goes against the Founder's Handbook, they are subject to believing the deceptive lies of Satan, and they will be led down a path of death, hell, and destruction!

In His Handbook, the Founder shows us how to defend ourselves from the wiles of Satan and his demon employees. Our Boss prepared us by way of His Handbook because He knew that there would come a time when the rebel and His followers would plot to take over His company. This is why it is important for God's employees to understand and agree with all the policies, terms, and conditions of the Bible.

Before the Founder *highers* a new employee, these terms and conditions must be agreed upon. Once you humbly agree and commit, you have a contract that lasts forever with the Founder of the company. This contract helps to ensure that there are no imposters who can breach the security of the company. If any employee refuses to pledge his or her commitment to the terms and conditions of the company, they will be in jeopardy of losing their company benefits and retirement plan and ultimately be fired! This statement can be verified in Romans 13:1–2 (KJV; emphasis added):

> Let every soul be subject to the higher powers [God, Jesus, and the Holy Spirit]. For there is no power but God: the powers that be are ordained of God. Whoever therefore resisteth the power, resisteth the ordinance of God: and they that resist shall receive to themselves damnation [or eternal hell].

This scripture informs us that everybody is subject to the higher powers, the Godhead, and there is no power on this earth but God. All power belongs to God! All other powers are subject to the Founder's wrath, judgment, and destruction. Any person who goes against God's plan will be dealt with severely. Know this, the Founder will never lead you to do anything bad for you. Everything that He planned for you is for your good. So, you must trust Him with your life and surrender your all to Him, withholding nothing.

Now we will explain why the Founder chose His Son as the CEO of His company. As you already know, God started the company, heaven and earth, simply by His spoken word for the sole purpose of creating humankind in His likeness and giving us dominion over every living thing. However, when Adam and Eve fell into sin, they offered unto God a substitutionary blood sacrifice of animals as an act of forgiveness for their sins. However, this Old Testament method for atonement was only a temporary fix to the ongoing problem of humankind's fallen state, because it had to be repeated over and over. Thus, it had no lasting power to save, deliver, or set us free from a mindset and lifestyle of sin.

Therefore, God had to come to earth in the form of human flesh through His Son Jesus, CEO, as a bodily sacrificial offering, by dying on the cross once and for all humankind to redeem us from sin, death, and eternal hell. Notice that I said Jesus only had to die one time. So those who believe and obey God and His Son will receive salvation and eternal life through Jesus Christ. This also means that their sins will be forgiven, and they will be new creatures in Him. The scriptural references that these statements are based on are found in Hebrews 5:9 (KJV; emphasis added):

> And having been perfected, He became the author of eternal salvation to all who obey Him.

Then, in Hebrews 5:26 (KJV), it is written (emphasis added),

> He then would have had to suffer often since the foundation of the world; but now, once at the end of the ages, He has appeared to put away sin by the sacrifice of Himself.

For that reason, the Founder made provisions for the one whom He chose to take over the company while He was creating more mansions in heaven. The one to take over the company was His Son, Jesus, whom He loved very dearly. The Son was the firstborn over all things, and the Founder was pleased to have everything that He is to dwell in Him (Jesus).

Jesus was created in the image of the Founder so much so that if you have seen Him, you have also seen the Founder. This scriptural reference is found in John 14:8–9 (NIV).

> Philip said, "Lord, show us the Father. That is all we need." Jesus replied:
>
> "Phillip, I have been with you for a long time. Don't you know who I am? If you have seen Me, you have seen the Father."

The only difference between the Founder and His Son is that Jesus appeared on earth in the flesh, and the Father (God) remained in Him in the Spirit. (Since the Son and the Father are one, when you have believed and obeyed the Son, you then automatically believe and obey the Father.) One reason why Jesus was ordained CEO of the earthly company was His obedience and love toward the Father. Everything Jesus did was to please His Father. Jesus demonstrated this from the smallest of deeds to the greatest, even to the point of sacrificing His very own life for the employees of the company on earth. Jesus was so committed that the Founder taught Him everything about running the company successfully, holding nothing back. Then God made Jesus heir over everything that He owned in heaven and on earth.

Now the Son was a dedicated disciple of everything that the Founder taught Him. Before long, His life would become the model for all humankind to follow. This would not be an easy task for Jesus to accomplish because many would doubt that He is even the Son of the Father, let alone believe that the Father sent Him into the world to save them from their sins. Nevertheless, it is written in the Handbook that anyone who does not respect the Son will be in danger of eternal damnation. Considering this fact, you must respect Jesus, for if the Founder ever heard otherwise, then you could be fired, literally, or even worse, sent to hell for being insubordinate and disrespectful to the Son. The Bible emphatically says in John 14:6 (NIV),

> Jesus answered, "I am the way and the truth and the life. No one comes to the Father except through Me."

Then, in John 5:22–23 (NKJV), it is written,

> For the Father judges no one, but has committed all judgment to the Son, that all should honor the Son just as they honor the Father. He who does not honor the Son does not honor the Father who sent Him.

Also, John 17:3 (NIV) states (emphasis added),

> And this is eternal life that they may know You, the only true God, and Jesus Christ whom You have sent.

All employees should endeavor to honor the Son as encouraged in the Handbook, not for the sole purpose of avoiding hell but so that our life can reflect the love, kindness, respect, understanding, forgiveness, and patience He has so graciously shown toward us. If Jesus demonstrated all these great attributes, then He desires that we do the same toward one another as fellow employees of His Father's company.

The love, commitment, and compassion the Son so graciously demonstrated to all humankind has gone down in history as one of the most heroic, humbling, and courageous acts that has ever been recorded in the history of the world!

Jesus possessed a love that He was willing to die for in that He unselfishly laid down His own life to redeem us from our sins. The anointing that the Founder placed on Jesus's life was nothing short of remarkable. Despite being mocked, hated, rejected, abandoned, forsaken, misunderstood, and even beaten to death, He willingly loved and forgave everyone unconditionally, refusing to repay evil with evil. Do you know that God's love for you is constant and never ending? According to 1 King 8:23 (MSG), Solomon uttered this prayer to God: "There is no God like you in the skies above or on the earth below who unswervingly keeps covenant with his servants and relentlessly loves them as they sincerely live in obedience to your way." In other words, Jesus has a relentless love for you and me that is unbreakable, unshakeable, unchangeable, and undeniable! So you don't ever have to worry about His love running out; He won't ever give up on you! His love will chase you out of dark places and captivate your heart. Once you grab a hold of His love, you'll never be the same!

> **Jesus has a relentless love for you and me that is unbreakable, unshakeable, unchangeable, and undeniable!**

People from the very elite to the extremely poor sought Him because of the extraordinary miracles they had observed Him perform. They sought Jesus for many different reasons, such as to heal the sick; to raise the dead; to call dry bones to be put back together; to cast out demons that encompassed the minds and bodies of some people; to heal blindness, deafness, and dumb spirits; to fill empty wine vats during wedding ceremonies; and to speak encouraging messages to the people. There were so many testimonies and rumors of some of the miraculous things that He did around the cities of Nazareth and Galilee. You may have read or heard about some of these accounts during your youth or adulthood. Many of you have even found these miraculous accounts hard to believe.

One testimony that stood out in the Handbook was that of the blind man found in John 9:1–41. As Jesus was walking throughout Jerusalem, He saw a man who had been blind from birth, and He asked the blind man, "Do you want to see?" When the blind man replied yes, Jesus spat in some mud, rubbed the man's eyes with the mixture, and soon after that, the man's eyesight was restored. When Jesus sees your condition and offers a solution to your problem, will you let him heal you? If you have never had an encounter with Jesus similar to that of the blind man in the Bible, I encourage you to stretch your faith, and invite Him in your situation. Remember this: there are some problems in life that He alone can fix.

Also, In Mark 3:1–5, another prominent story told was of Jesus healing a man with a withered right hand. The significance of emphasizing his right hand was due to the fact that most people during that time were right-hand dominant. Consequently, this meant that this man was physically handicapped or disabled, which made it impossible for him to work and make a decent living to support himself. When Jesus saw that the man's right hand was shriveled up and couldn't move, He commanded the man to "stretch out your hand." Jesus told the man to do something that he couldn't do in his own strength. But by *faith* in Jesus's word, the man stretched out his hand, and immediately, it was restored like the other one. This story illustrates that, at the command of Jesus, there is *enabling power* if we simply act in faith upon what He commands us to do. The victory is won by faith in the finished work of the cross. Anything that a person does is done by faith because it takes faith in Jesus's word to move the heart of God! Do you have the kind of faith to stop Jesus in His tracks? As you can see from the examples in this book, He wants to heal, deliver, and set the captives free, which takes faith to do it.

There are many eyewitness events like these all throughout the Bible. Another favorite is found in Mark 5:25–34, about a woman who had an issue with bleeding for twelve long years and whose faith was born in desperation. This woman had gone to see many doctors for a chronic abnormal condition (possibly a fibroid tumor of the uterus) that caused her personal embarrassment. This was a condition that she felt due to chronic loss of blood, which probably caused her to be anemic and physically fatigued. Additionally, the cost of her ongoing medical treatments depleted all her financial savings. She knew that under the doctor's care, nothing was working—her money and friends were gone, and her health was getting worse.

One day, she heard about the Son coming to her town. With all the challenges the woman experienced (incapable of being healed), she thought, *If I could just touch the hem of His garment*, I would be made whole. Her strong belief in Jesus's power to heal her caused her to break social taboos regarding unclean people—they had to be isolated from society and were not allowed to attend worship services. But once she had it in her spiritual heart that Jesus could heal her, *nothing* was able to stop her. Of necessity, when she saw her opportunity, she pressed her way through a large crowd of people who also wanted to see Jesus. According to this archived event, she crawled on her hands and knees through the crowd with people stepping on her fingers, shoving, pressing against, and falling on her while dust particles were getting in her eyes, ears, nose, and mouth. (Just imagine being in this woman's shoes. Would you have liked being trampled on by a crowd of people? Certainly not! But when you want something bad enough, you will possess an unstoppable faith like this woman did. Then, you must release yourself to the only one who can correct your condition.) Nevertheless, through it all, she still continued to press on to touch the hem of the Son's garment. At the moment of touching His hem, her bleeding immediately stopped, and the woman was *instantly* healed. (Praise almighty God!)

What was more bizarre was that when the woman touched Jesus, He turned around to see who touched Him. It could have been anyone in the crowd because there were so many people gathered there to see Him. He was literally touched in His Spirit by the faith of the person who touched Him. The person's faith was so strong that Jesus felt some of His power leave His body. Excited and curious, Jesus called out aloud, "Who touched me?"

At the sound of His voice, the woman became afraid because no woman was to touch the Son or any other man of authority in public. Company policy did not allow such intrusion upon anyone in upper management, and that act alone could lead to public shame or, even worse, death by stoning. The woman humbled herself and spoke out, letting Jesus know she was the person who had touched His garment. Jesus then confidently proclaimed to the obedient employee, the woman, and to the rest of the world, "It was your faith that has healed you, daughter, be freed from your suffering." This is an example of true worship of the Son and courageous faith on the part of the woman. Additionally, this shows genuine love and concern toward the woman on the part of Jesus. Can you exhibit a faith that is born in desperation like this woman did? Oftentimes, it takes crazy faith to get God's attention!

The Handbook points to another account found in John 2:1–11, in which the Son was at a wedding with His earthly mother in Cana of Galilee and the bride's father ran out of wine for the wedding feast.

Mary, the mother of Jesus, asked Him to do something about the shortage of wine. Jesus was hesitant at first and stated to His mother that His time had not yet come, but Mary perceived that his time was near for His purpose on Earth to be fulfilled. What happened next was the first of the Son's many miracles to come.

The Son then sent the servants to get some large wine vats and fill them with water. The servants did as Jesus had instructed. Once the Son lifted His eyes to heaven and blessed the vats, He told the servants to take the vats to the father of the bride and have Him taste it. The father was amazed at how good the second collection of wine tasted, the wine that Jesus made and blessed. This surprisingly amazed the father of the bride because it was customary to serve the finest wine first then the least expensive wine last. Can you envision the expression of bewilderment and disbelief on the faces of all who witnessed this miracle? I wish I could have been there to witness this miracle myself!

There are so many inspiring stories resembling these throughout the Handbook that you may read and meditate upon during your personal time. As you can see, the basis for Jesus coming to earth was to show us by example how to love one another and live to please the Founder God. In essence, He came to set the captives free!

While Jesus performed many miracles and walked among His disciples, He suffered many things, including threats to end His life from those who hated Him. For this reason, in John 14:1–3 (NIV), He informed His disciples that He would soon be departing to be "highered" or elevated to be with the Father by saying to them,

> Do not let your hearts be troubled. You believe in God; believe also in Me. My Father's house has many rooms; if that were not so, would I have told you that I am going to prepare a place for you? And if I go and prepare a place for you, I will come back and take you to be with Me, that you also may be where I am.

As a safety measure, the Founder placed in the Handbook what steps to take in case His Son's physical life should come to an end. The Founder stated in the Handbook that if, for any reason, Jesus was fatally injured in an accident or murdered, the next in line to fill in for the CEO position would be the Holy Spirit (a.k.a., the GM). In all honesty, the Founder *knew* that His Son was going to be crucified, so it wasn't an issue of "just in case" but a matter of *when*. Hence, the Son had to prepare the employees of the Founder for His death and teach them about the third person of the Godhead.

The Holy Spirit, which is the third body or person of the Godhead, came into existence after the death and resurrection of Jesus to lead, guide, and comfort God's employees and to help them accomplish the company's mission. The responsibility of the Holy Spirit is to bring to the remembrance of God's employees the truths they have learned about the Founder (John 14:26). After the Holy Spirit comes upon a person, that person receives understanding about spiritual things, and he or she possesses power to witness to people all over the world, and from *diverse* religions, about the power of God in a believer's life (read Acts 1:8).

If you want to increase your understanding of God and His truth, you must get deeper in God by reading His Handbook, praying, attending a local fellowship of believers, creating an environment of praise and worship in your home, and befriending other believers. Once the Holy Spirit comes into the heart and mind of a person, He abides with and guides them (Romans 8:14, John 14:16–18). He teaches them all things and how to pray (John 14:26; Romans 8:26). He reminds them of the Word (John 14:26). He heals them based on their faith (Romans 8:11).

The Holy Spirit tells them of things to come (John 16:13). He declares to them the things of Jesus (John 16:12–15). He empowers them to be witnesses of the Good News (Acts 1:8). He encourages them to live a solid Christian lifestyle and endows them with the power to stop doing corrupt things, such as lying, fornicating, gossiping, and abusing alcohol and drugs (Ephesians 4:22–32). Acts 1:8 (NIV) pronounces,

> But you will receive power when the Holy Spirit comes on you, and you will be My witnesses in Jerusalem, in all Judea and Samaria, and to the ends of the earth.

The Founder God created humankind to bring Him and His Son's name honor and glory. His mission was to redeem you from your sins through the life, death, and resurrection of Jesus Christ. Upon Jesus's death, the Holy Spirit was sent as the *active force* from heaven to give us wisdom to make good decisions in every aspect of our lives, knowledge to know what to do and how to pray, power to live a victorious life in Christ, and comfort in times of trouble.

> **Once the Holy Spirit comes into the heart and mind of a person, He abides with and guides them.**

Those of you who choose to obey and follow the Founder's principles and instructions through the Holy Spirit will have an abundant life on earth and eternal life in heaven. The only way your life can be harmed, destroyed, and sent to hell is when you yield to the temptations of the flesh, the world, and Satan and willfully refuse to repent of your sins. The Bible is the infallible Word of God, where we get answers to all life's questions.

Although the methods may change, the principles of the Handbook—the Bible, that is—will always remain the same throughout the history of heaven and earth. By following the Founder's Handbook, you will receive His benefits of blessings, favor, guidance, protection, love, peace, joy, and comfort at all times. You will also learn your A, B, C's—Always Be Christlike. Later in the book, you will learn more about the fate of the first rebel and those who wanted to follow him and his ideas.

*My son, do not associate with rebels.*

—Proverbs 24:21 (NLT)

# Chapter 3

## True Employment— Jesus's Job Announcement

For centuries, the gospel has been pronounced all over the earth by such television pastors, evangelists, and missionaries as Mother Teresa, Martin Luther King Jr., Gandhi, Billy Graham, and still today, Dr. Tony Evans and Dr. Charles Stanley, in an effort to teach moral and spiritual principles to help people fulfill their divine purpose here on earth, as well as to win lost souls to Christ. Getting highered has been the biggest and best news spread since the days of Jesus Christ! During the era in which Jesus walked the earth, countless men, women, and children lined up to hear Him discuss the many job openings that were available in the Founder's company and to advise them about how to get highered. His appeal was to crowds of people who wanted more out of life than just the normal day-to-day experience of dealing with problems. The kind of people who followed Jesus were mostly enthused applicants who wanted to fulfill a meaningful purpose in life.

Jesus came to earth to provide hope to all humankind by offering repentance, forgiveness of sins, and eternal salvation. Moreover, Jesus's mission on earth included training us for missionary work, evangelism, and baptism to become His disciples. His training has also helped humankind solve many challenging problems in life—such as healing terminally-ill people on whom the doctors have given up, casting out demonic forces or curing mental confusion in patients whom many psychologists and psychiatrists cannot help, and appealing to the greedy, self-centered hearts of the rich to compel them to be compassionate and generous in meeting the needs of the poor, widows, and orphans.

Jesus's presence here on earth was not intended to exempt us from experiencing pain, suffering, and disappointments but to teach us how to live lovingly among one another so we all could accomplish the Great Commission. He successfully got the Word out back then, and now, with all the advancements made available to us through technology, we can spread the gospel throughout the world instantaneously by a simple text message from our cellular phones or by a click of the mouse from our computers. In the last quarter of the twentieth century, due to the increase of worldwide calamities—such as terrorism; bank fraud and failures; divorce and same-sex marriages, which attack the traditional family unit; unemployment; poverty; hunger; abortions; mass murders; teen suicides; hurricanes; and the spread of HIV/AIDS; and currently, the Corona Virus (COVID 19) pandemic and the shutting down of churches, schools, and businesses—many people have become interested in learning about how to obtain spiritual employment. As a result of fear deriving from these catastrophic world events and distrust in the current policy makers of the world, the heart of humankind has returned to the Founder's mission: "to seek and to save that which was lost." This statement is long-established by the scripture reference found in Luke 19:10 (KJV):

For the Son of man is come to seek and to save that which was lost.

The Founder God knew ahead of time that He would have enough business to employ at least a hundred billion employees at one time to achieve the mission of His company. That may sound like scores of job openings, but we serve a bigtime Boss who thinks big! Besides, every successful business entrepreneur is admired and praised for his or her ability to think outside the box. One attribute of employment that employees of the Founder say they like most about God is His business savvy.

Currently, there are approximately 7 billion people living on planet Earth, and that total is growing at a rate of approximately 80 million per year (Grist 2010). Christianity is the largest religion in the world today with thirty-eight thousand denominations worldwide and approximately 2 billion believers, or 33 percent of the world's population. Of these 2 billion Christians, 648 million (11 percent of the world's population) are Evangelicals or Bible-believing Christians, with 54 percent being nonwhites.

There are 20,500 full-time Christian workers and 10,200 foreign missionaries actively involved in the unevangelized world, and 1.31 million full-time Christian workers participating in the evangelized non-Christian world. According to the census.gov report, there are 311 million Christians or 78 percent of adult believers in the United States today, which makes it the largest Christian population on earth. The *Yearbook of American and Canadian Churches* and the National Council of Churches sited the five largest denominations in America as the following: The Catholic Church, the Southern Baptist Convention, the United Methodist Church, the Church of Jesus Christ of Latter-day Saints, and the Church of God in Christ (*Christianity Today* 2005).

Christianity originated with Jesus and has spread throughout the world in many forms of religion, yet there are still many opportunities available to you for spiritual employment to spread the gospel. This implies that there is a great supply of available job openings for anyone who is highered and willing to work for the Founder. Employees who work for the Founder can have more than one job depending on their God-given spiritual gifts. So don't be deceived, heaven is highering, and the abundance of jobs within the Founder's company is limitless!

With one hundred billion job openings, there are a lot of choices as to what kind of work you can do in the Founder's company, such as evangelizing, going on missions, preaching, teaching, joining the help ministry during disasters, praising and worshiping, dancing, and singing, and so forth. It would please the Founder to see all one hundred billion jobs immediately filled so that He could start more franchises in different places. The increase in franchises would create a great demand to fill more job positions, which means that the Boss would have to higher more employees. This kind of growth and development are signs of a flourishing economy, and the Founder enjoys seeing His company expand.

What is better than observing the company prosper is observing the employees perform their duties with an attitude of gratitude. Other than finding qualified candidates based on related skills and experience, most earthly employers find that highering an employee with a positive attitude helps create a happy and healthy work environment. Like earthly employers who appreciate employees with a winning attitude, the Founder is looking to higher and reward people who work hard and do their service for the company without grumbling and complaining. The gifts that He gives are priceless, and yet He gives generously to all employees who please Him with their hard work ethic, and positive attitude. In Philippians 2:14 (NKJV), the apostle Paul admonished his congregation to do the following:

> Do all things without complaining and disputing, that you may become blameless and harmless, children of God without fault in the midst of a crooked and perverse generation, among whom you shine as lights in the world, holding fast the word of life, so that I may rejoice in the day of Christ that I have not run in vain or labored in vain.

It is essential that all employees of the Founder's company exercise diligence and a spirit of excellence in all that they do in representing God so that those who are not highered as of yet would want to become a part of the Founder's company.

There are other reasons why a person would want to be highered with the Founder's company. One of the most important reasons is to receive immediate benefits. After the interview is complete and they agree to the company policies and agreement clause (which will be discussed in the next chapter), they are immediately highered in the company.

Once you have agreed to the Founder's terms and conditions of the Handbook, there is no waiting period to process your application or any background checks. Unlike earthly companies, the Founder does not consult your past to determine your future in His company. He throws your past in the sea of forgetfulness, never to be used against you again (read Micah 7:19). God's mercy gives you a clean slate to start afresh. He knew your tendency toward sin before He formed you in your mother's womb, and yet He separated you to be a prophet (a messenger) unto this nation (read Jeremiah 1:5 NIV).

Several important attributes that the Founder looks for in a potential employee are his or her willingness to submit to His authority, willingness to become a lifelong disciple (learner) of Christ, and willingness to comply with company policies. To do this, you must be saved. The Founder *spiritually employs* or saves you by grace through faith alone, and your willingness to "confess with your mouth the Lord Jesus and believe in your heart that God has raised you from the dead, and then you shall be saved" (Romans 10:9 NIV). Also, to be saved and maintain salvation with the Founder, you must repent of your sins. To *repent* means to turn away from your sinful lifestyle and turn to God (read 1 Thessalonians 1:9).

Another definition of this term says,

> To turn away from any plan, system or teaching advocating salvation by works, such as good deeds, rituals or religious practices—turning to Christ as the [*only*] sacrifice for the sins of the Founder's creation. (BibleOne).

---

**Unlike earthly companies, the Founder does not consult your past to determine your future in His company.**

---

Please understand this: no one is saved merely by "good works" alone. If that were the case, then all the secular organizations such as sororities, fraternities, the Freemasons, and the Make-A-Wish Foundation, which practice good works would all be saved based on their good deeds. Thus, there would be no need for anyone involved in charitable organizations to strive for heaven.

This is worth saying: insanity is at its worst when the creature thinks he is greater than the Creator. But God (in His infinite wisdom) will have no other gods before Him. Humankind's best works could *never* be accomplished by its efforts alone due to the sacrifice Jesus made at Calvary. My previous point is worth reemphasizing: God would *never* make Himself *unnecessary* in the life of His own creation. In this case, both employees and nonemployees are all created by Him. However, it is only through the *grace* of God that He assists His employees to do His good work of salvation. This statement is backed up by four scripture verses first written in Ephesians 2:8–9 (KJV; emphasis added):

> For by grace are ye saved through faith; and that not of yourselves: it is the gift of God: not of works, lest any man should boast.

Then in Ephesians 2:10 (KJV), it is written,

> For we are His workmanship, created in Christ Jesus unto good works, which God hath before ordained that we should walk in them.

Also, in Titus 3:5 (KJV), it is written,

> Not by works of righteousness which we have done, but according to His mercy He saved us, by the washing of regeneration, and renewing of the Holy Ghost.

> **Insanity is at its worst when the creature thinks he is greater than the Creator. But God (in His infinite wisdom) will have no other gods before Him.**

Contrary to earthly company policies, the Founder's job requirements are not based on your earthly job history, educational references, criminal background, credit checks, fingerprints, or drug tests. You don't have to have a perfect past nor a long title behind your name nor be affiliated with the got-it-going-on social club to become an employee of the

Founder. You see, Matthew 28:19–20 (KJV) pronounced that before you chose to join the Founder's company, He had already chosen you to be highered for His great work to do the following:

> Go ye therefore, and teach all the nations, baptizing them in the name of the Father, and of the Son, and of the Holy Spirit. Teaching them to observe all that I have commanded you; and, lo, I am with you always, even to the end of the world. Amen.

Every time you go anywhere, all you have to do is say *that* name. The name of Jesus has *exousia* power! This means that Jesus's name has absolute power, might-and-wonder-working power! *That* name is to be heralded everywhere you go throughout the hedges and highways to compel the lost sheep to God the Father! Romans 10:13 (KJV) exclaims, "For whosoever shall call upon the name of the Lord shall be saved."

When a person calls on the name of Jesus, he or she takes on new employment with the Founder's company and is being *elevated* in the spirit. That is why the Founder enjoys highering as many employees who desire to follow Him.

In His great wisdom and understanding, the Founder skillfully selected the title for this book—*Heaven Is Highering*—because He knew that this motto would grasp the attention of humankind in relation to his understanding of earthly employment.

When you saw this title, you probably thought that the word *highering* was misspelled, but here is what the Founder wants to share with you. Instead, humankind has misspelled the words *hire*, *hiring*, and *hired*. Humankind, according to *Merriam-Webster*, defines the words *hire*, *hiring*, and *hired* as thus:

> "to grant the personal services of or temporary use of for a fixed sum; to take employment; the state of being hired."

Although humans were correct with the basic underlying meaning of employment, they missed the literal understanding of employment when they omitted the meaning of the word high. According to *Webster*, this is the meaning of the word *high*:

"at or to a high place, altitude, or degree; an elevated place or region; the space overhead—sky or heaven."

When you place together the meanings of the two words defined by humankind—*high and hiring*—then you have a better understanding of the true meaning of *highering* as defined by the Founder: *to be elevated in the spirit.* This spiritual elevation brings us closer to the Founder, God the Father. It is only when we are elevated in the spirit that we can see and understand the Founder, His Handbook, things that are happening in the world and His plan for our lives. As long as you are in your natural state of mind, you cannot comprehend spiritual things. Spiritual things can only be conceived by cultivating a personal relationship with God. These statements are validated by the following scriptural references in 1 Corinthians 2:14–16 (KJV; emphasis added):

> But the natural man receiveth not the things of the Spirit of God: for they are foolishness unto him: neither can he know them because they are Spiritually discerned. But he that is Spiritual judgeth all things, yet he himself is judged of no man. For who hath known the mind of the Lord, that he may instruct him? But we have the mind of Christ.

For example, the first two original employees on earth were Adam and Eve. They were in perfect communion with the Founder—that is, until they decided to take employment matters into their own hands and disobeyed the Founder by eating the fruit that was forbidden. In doing this one act, they violated one of the sacred company rules and regulations. (Their account of disobedience and the consequences that followed are documented in the Founder's Handbook.) Immediately after Adam and Eve disobeyed God, they caused all creation after them to be cut off from receiving all the benefits that God created for them. They also had their earthly retirement plan revoked because now they had to physically work for everything. However, all was not lost. Because of His mercy and grace toward humankind, the Founder gave us another chance to become spiritually employed through the confession of Jesus as Lord and Savior and through the forgiveness of sins. Someone once said, "Where God makes a promise, He always makes a provision." Surprisingly enough, however, I have learned that

God's promise comes with a condition. In other words, Jesus is the provision that brings God's promise to pass in your life. So, to possess the promise, you must accept the provision—Jesus Christ. Then you will have everything you need to possess the promises of God. God is so good to make a way for our redemption through His Son!

> **Jesus is the provision that brings God's promise to pass in your life.**

The Founder has commissioned all His creation, including you, to proclaim the gospel throughout the world, especially now that we have all the technological advances to do so. There are many job positions that He has available for employment, such as evangelizing, mission work, praise and worship, singing and dancing, intercessory prayer, counseling, writing books, and feeding and taking care of the poor, orphans, and widows. He has given you one or more spiritual gifts that can be used to promote His company. This is an invitation for you to come aboard as an employee of the company and utilize your gifts to compel others to Christ, as well as to receive the greatest benefits package that you'll ever have on earth and in heaven. Spiritual employment and the gift of eternal life can be yours today! Applications can be obtained and completed in the next chapter.

> *For I am not ashamed of the gospel of Christ: for it is the power of God unto salvation to everyone that believeth: the Jew first, and also the Greek.*

—Romans 1:16 (KJV)

# Chapter 4

## How to Apply for Spiritual Employment

When the Founder laid the ground rules for employment, He made the application process simple and easy, enough for even a child to understand. This way, no one would have an excuse as to why they could not get highered with the Founder's company. Just as an earthly employer seeks applicants who are looking to settle into a particular career path, the Founder is seeking applicants who are serious about devoting themselves to a lifetime calling with His company. To attract serious-minded candidates for employment, the Founder has set essential characteristics that all applicants must possess at the time of application, or at least be willing to develop, as they journey along in their Christian walk.

All the attributes that will be named below are a part of the application process for the Founder's company and are necessary for spiritual employment.

The first criteria, which must be met prior to your decision to apply and work for the Founder, requires love, trust, faith, hope, forgiveness, and thankfulness. As an employee of the Founder, you will be required to harmoniously work on a team because no person is an island in and of him or herself. Just as an earthly employer expects his employees to get along with one another in order to reach their full potential and target the goals and objectives of the corporation, the Founder expects you to maintain a team spirit in His company too. To be effective and efficient at working together, all these attributes named above are to be applied daily as you strive to build, comfort, and support one another by way of the Holy Spirit that lives in you.

Of all the scriptural references quoted in the Bible, Jesus mentioned love as the first and greatest attribute of all humankind. If you *love* others, then you can trust them too. If you trust others, then you will have faith in them too. If you have *faith* in them, then you will *hope* the best for them too. If you hope the best for them, then you will forgive them for their imperfections too. If you can *forgive* them, then you can be *thankful* for their presence in your life too. This statement can be verified in 1 Corinthians 13:4–8 (NIV; emphasis added):

> Love is patient, love is kind. It does not envy, it does not boast, it is not proud. It does not dishonor others, it is not self-seeking, it is not easily angered, it keeps no record of wrongs [doesn't bring up the past]. Love does not delight in evil but rejoices [thankfully] with the truth. It always protects, trusts, hopes, and perseveres. Love never fails.

---

**"Outside of the nucleus of love, no relationship can possibly survive." (Victoria Livingston-Johnson)**

---

My wife, Victoria, coined the quote. Therefore, the significance of the Founder placing more emphasis on love than any other attribute is this: without love, absolutely nothing can survive! Marriages, business partnerships, the raising of children, ministries, and the like would not be possible without love. This, in turn, means that trust, faith, hope, forgiveness, thankfulness, and other good qualities cannot be fulfilled without expressing genuine love toward others. To love someone means that you trust them because you cannot love someone you don't trust and vice versa. You cannot receive or discover the true beauty of God's love without trust.

On the other hand, it is true that a person can have head knowledge and use it to impress many people, but without heart love toward others, it profits him or her nothing. This statement is endorsed by the scripture reference found in 1 Corinthians 13:1–3 (KJV; emphasis added):

> Though I speak with the tongues of men and of angels, and have not charity [love], I am become as sounding brass, or a tinkling cymbal. And though I have the gift of prophecy, and understand all mysteries, and all knowledge; and though I have all faith, so that I could remove mountains, and have not charity, I am nothing. And though I bestow all my goods to feed the poor, and though I give my body to be burned, and have not charity, it profiteth me nothing.

---

**You cannot receive or discover the true beauty of God's love without trust.**

---

Tina Turner, one of the most renowned pop singers of this generation, sang a popular song in the '80s entitled "What's Love Got to Do With It." As you can see from the all-inclusive Handbook, love has everything to do with our lives on earth as it is in heaven. Tina and Ike Turner were materially wealthy because they used their God-given musical talents; however, they suffered an impoverished love life that caused a violent divorce. Case in point, jealousy and envy toward the gift of sharing a marriage and business partnership together will block the blessings of love, trust, faith, and hope that is intended to come from the marital union—just as Ike's jealousy spoiled everything with Tina.

Being thankful can lead to bountiful blessings of love and deep commitments within relationships. Love is the ingredient that makes life meaningful and relationships wealthy. True wealth is not defined by how rich you are, but how well you love. To God, wealth is a spiritual concept, not a physical one because it can only come into existence when you put love into action. How well do you love others? For without love, you are nothing, and your divine purpose for existing would literally be destroyed. Always remember that without God and people to share life with, you're spiritually poor.

> **Love is the ingredient that makes life meaningful and relationships wealthy.**
>
> ---
>
> **True wealth is not defined by how rich you are, but by how well you love.**

The second criteria, which must be met prior to your decision to apply and work for the Founder, requires you to be ready, willing, and able to deny yourself daily and become a disciple or lifelong student of the Handbook. According to Luke 9:23 (NKJV),

> Then He [Jesus] said to them all, "If anyone desires to come after Me, let him deny himself, and take up his cross daily, and follow Me."

Also, in 2 Timothy 2:12 (KJV), it is written,

> If we suffer, we shall also reign with Him: if we deny him, He also will deny us.

For Jesus to accept and increase you, there must be a decrease and denial of yourself, your flesh, and the pleasures of the world. Taking up your cross isn't going to be easy because it will require much effort on your part to be tenacious enough to stand up for righteousness and holiness when times get tough, and I can assure you that you *will* face some bumps in the road during your Christian walk with Jesus. But you can still be joyful when your life is filled with trials, disappointments, pain, and suffering—for Jesus promised that you will not walk this life alone. For He declared this scripture in Matthew 28:20 (KJV; emphasis added):

> Teaching them [His disciples] to observe all things whatsoever I have commanded you: and, lo, *I am with you always*, even unto the end of the world.

Even though Jesus is no longer on the earth, it is encouraging to know that He is with us through the Handbook, the GM (Holy Spirit), and through our fellowshipping with other Christians. Accordingly, there is always help available to you in victoriously overcoming any problem that you'll ever face in life.

The third criteria, which must be met before you decide to apply and work for the Founder, requires a willingness to be humble, accountable, and responsible to God and to those whom God places in authority over you. First Peter 5:6 (KJV) instruct us to do the following:

> Humble yourselves therefore under the mighty hand of God, that He may exalt you in due time.

Because the world teaches people to get all you can while you can on your *own* terms, it is quite upsetting and troublesome to see how this greedy, self-gratifying, arrogant, and insensitive attitude has produced so many broken marriages and families, business and government feuds and failures, splits within churches, and irreconcilable relationships. Although our nation was founded on godly principles of faith, righteousness, and justice for all, the earthly leaders of today are passing laws that go against the very principles that our forefathers initially set forth in the constitution.

As a result of the lack of personal responsibility for one's actions, lack of accountability toward one another, and lack of honor toward godly principles—the walls of our communities and nation have broken down! Therefore, it is going to take much prayer and humility on our behalf to petition the Founder for mercy and grace to rebuild the broken walls of our homes, communities, and nation.

I would like to take this moment to elaborate on the job crisis in America today, which has affected many people due to the poor decisions made by upper management. With the great recession in the beginning of the twenty-first century upon us, the timing for these job openings (spiritual employment, that is) could not have come at a better time. Our days on earth are in peril, and our hearts grow heavy as we shoulder the weight of the economic crisis that has expanded across the globe.

America's fall in the industrial revolution will go down in history as a major economic turning point. This crash in the American economy became evident in 2008, when she experienced the financial collapse of big industries. It was so bad that the big three automakers in American history—General Motors, Ford, and Chrysler—went to the United States government and asked to borrow billions of dollars from us taxpayers to help them stay afloat and continue running their companies.

Each day, we hopelessly listened as the television, radio, and internet media reminded us constantly of the grim realities of America's economic disasters. News of more job losses became the genre of the day, and many of us grew faint with the fear of losing our jobs, if we had not already lost them. We were constantly bombarded with the statistics of the hundreds of thousands of us who had lost jobs and savings through voided 401(k) plans and other reneged retirement plans. Many American citizens and countless others throughout the world were robbed by the American government and large American-owned financial giants.

With the increase of moral decay in government, big business, big pharma, big agribiz, religion, and family, many of us have lost our families, our homes, our investments, our retirements, and our way of living. Some have become fearful, hopeless, and vulnerable—and have even lost their will to live.

The massive loss of jobs was caused by the domino effect of a crumbling stock market on Wall Street due to bad investments in the housing industry. These bad investments then led to bank failings and a large number of company closures. Included in this downfall were the largest and most well-known brokerage firms, which were forced to file for bankruptcy because of the real estate investments gone bad by government-backed agencies like Fannie Mae and Freddie Mac.

Irresponsibility seemed to run rampant in the too-big-to-fail companies. Due to the irresponsible actions of big corporations, hundreds of billions of dollars' worth of "unrecognized" bad debt came crashing down on the United States economy, and we taxpayers were, once again, expected to pick up the bill. You see, when the heads of corporations refuse to uphold godly principles, they deceptively *make* themselves blind to the future consequences that their poor choices will soon produce and, in turn, detrimentally affect the lives of many innocent people.

It's ironic that when the average citizen is late making payments on their mortgage, vehicle, college tuition, medical bills, or credit cards, they are punished with high-interest rates, either due to their irresponsible debt management or unforeseen circumstances that forced them to pick up an extra bill. However, this same punishment does not apply to the corporate giants. On the contrary, when these crooked too-big-to-fail companies make these same mistakes, they are rewarded for their irresponsibility while we taxpayers erroneously suffer and are forced to flip the bill for their financial mistakes as well as our own. This kind of atypical behavior is an example of modern-day financial slavery, alive and well in America and throughout the world! These are just a few examples of the poor decisions the upper management has made to tear down the foundation of our families, communities, and nation.

The Founder would *never* run a business like this! Besides, He is the Savior, protector, and supporter of all humankind, even, by His grace and mercy, to those who formerly made themselves corrupt. His very deity is to behave in a manner that represents holiness, righteousness, and justice in all matters. His reputation is much too important to get caught up in the lust for greed, filthy lucre, manipulation, power struggles, and such corruption that has many carnal-minded men and women entangled. In fact, no one can ever make the excuse that when he or she does evil, it was God who tempted him or her because God will *not* tempt anyone, nor can He be tempted. This statement can be confirmed in James 1:13 (NKJV):

> Let no one say when he is tempted, "I am tempted by God"; for God cannot be tempted by evil, nor does He Himself tempt anyone.

Therefore, it is impossible for the Founder to ever run such poorly managed companies as the too-big-to-fail corporations because God cannot be tempted to sin. Nor would He ever tempt anyone to do evil.

Quite the opposite, Jesus was tempted because He came to earth as God in human flesh. Due to the fact that Jesus was in his physical body, He had to use His five senses just as we do. He could both naturally and supernaturally see (vision), hear (discern), taste, smell, and touch (feel emotionally and physically), which was why his natural senses exposed Him to all sorts of temptations and provoked Him to resist and use self-control.

For example, in Matthew 4:1–11, after Jesus came out of the wilderness from fasting for forty days and nights, He was hungry. As soon as Jesus came out of His fast, He was approached by the tempter (Satan) three times to get Him to bow down and worship him. Satan knew that Jesus was hungry, tired, weak, and very vulnerable. Yet Satan timed his attempt perfectly and even used the Word of God to try to ensnare Jesus during His weakest moment. Nevertheless, Christ prevailed by referring to His Father, and quoting the Handbook, saying, "It is written." He was tempted in all points, yet He never sinned. This statement has been long established in Hebrews 4:15 (NIV; emphasis added):

> For we do not have a high priest [Jesus] who is unable to empathize with our weaknesses, but we have one who has been tempted in every way, just as we are—yet he did not sin.

Also, 1 Peter 2:21–22 (NKJV) declares (emphasis added),

> For to this you were called, because Christ also suffered for us, leaving us an example, that you should follow His steps: Who committed no sin nor was deceit found in His mouth.

Then there is 1 John 3:5–6 (NKJV), which says (emphasis added),

> And you know that He was manifested to take away our sins, and in Him there is no sin.

The reason Jesus did not sin when He was tempted was that "God was in Him reconciling the world to Himself" (read 1 Corinthians

5:12). Suffice it to say that when there is no sin found in a person, only righteousness is present.

> **When there is no sin found in a person, only righteousness is present.**

In a world with so many corrupt politicians, drug dealers, arms dealers, and those who fleece and exploit the world, it is no surprise that there is so much misery and chaos running rampant throughout the entire planet. It was *never* the Founder's plan or intention for His employees to be abused by upper management. Earthly managers were supposed to be good stewards over *all* whom the Founder entrusted to them on earth. They were instructed by the Founder to protect His investments and look out for the best interest of His employees. Instead, they have taken food from the mouths of the Founder's employees and robbed them of their promotions, job security, benefits, and retirement plans.

As a result of the increase in dishonesty with one another, broken (business) contracts, company theft, greed, and lust for money and power, it has become more difficult to trust authority on the earth. These issues of lying, cheating, and deceiving one another have caused a vast increase in demand for lawyers to mediate in the courtrooms because of irresponsibility, unkept promises, broken contracts, and broken marital covenants. However, the Handbook is clear on how to solve such corruption. The Founder stated in 2 Chronicles 7:14 (NKJV; emphasis added),

> If my people, who are called by my name, will *humble* themselves and *pray* and *seek* my face and *turn* from their wicked ways, then I will hear from heaven and forgive their sin and heal their land.

Then, in James 4:7, 10 (KJV), He instructs,

> *Submit* [be accountable and responsible] yourselves therefore to God. Resist the devil, and he will flee from you. Humble yourselves in the sight of the Lord, and He shall lift you up.

These scriptures promise that if you—upper management, politicians, corporate leaders, military officials, religious leaders, doctors, educators, husbands, wives, singles, and children—submit yourselves to God and spiritual authority, the walls of our nation will be rebuilt, our land will be healed, and our sins *will* be forgiven! It is vital that we all uphold the principles of the Founder in order to regain a loving, trustworthy, humble, accountable, honorable, and faithful nation under God. Applying these characteristics to our daily lives will significantly increase the moral and spiritual integrity of our nation, communities, churches, and homes.

The fourth and final criteria require endurance, loyalty, faithfulness, and commitment from you to maintain spiritual-employment status with the Founder's company. There will be many days in your life when you will be tested by Satan; by the doctrines of the scribes and Pharisees of long ago (whom Jesus referred to as serpents and a brood of vipers because they were outwardly religious but were *inwardly* haters of Christ in Matthew 23:33); by negative thoughts; by old sinful habits, which will try to creep into your life; and even by unsaved relatives, old friends, and associates who are not good role models. Moreover, because our culture conditions us to depend on yourself (self-sufficiency) and others in your sphere of influence (codependency), there will be many battles in your mind (spiritual heart) that will come to confuse and tempt you to give up your Christian walk.

Although we are not islands in and of ourselves, God created us to find our core sufficiency in Him alone for us to become faithful, loyal, and committed servants. The reason God instructed us not to put our trust in people is because, at some point in our lives, people will let us down. Even well-meaning family and friends will turn their backs on us for serving God. God is the only true source who will ever supply all our needs according to His glorious riches in Christ Jesus (Philippians 4:19). Thus, such habits of self-dependency and codependency can be difficult to break away from, but it's *not* impossible. For God said in Luke 10:19 (KJV),

> Behold, I give unto you power to tread on serpents and scorpions, and over all the power of the enemy [Satan and his hosts]: and nothing shall by any means hurt you.

Then, in 1 Corinthians 10:13 (NKJV), it is written (emphasis added),

> *No* temptation has overtaken you except such as is common to man; but God is faithful, who will not allow you to be tempted beyond what you are able, but with the temptation will also make the way of escape, that you may be able to bear it.

As you spiritually grow more like Jesus, He gives you power through the Holy Spirit to victoriously overcome bad habits, negative thoughts, wrong relationships, and any temptation that you will ever go through. By reading and meditating on the Handbook daily, you will find answers to any problem you will face in life and learn what to do and say about various issues. Joshua 1:8 (NKJV) instructs you to do as follows:

> This book of the law shall not depart from your mouth, but you shall [*meditate*] on it day and night, so that you may be careful to do according to all that is written in it; for then you will make your way prosperous, and then you will have good success.

As you can see, being loyal, faithful, and committed to the Founder will help you endure many trials in life. These attributes will also assist you in being promoted to a *higher* level once you have proven that you are truly faithful over little tasks. They will also help you enter into the joy of the Lord. The Handbook makes this declaration in Matthew 25:21 (KJV):

> His lord said unto him, "Well done, thou good and faithful servant: thou hast been faithful over a few things, I will make thee ruler over many things: enter thou into the joy of thy Lord."

The Founder designed biblical criteria for humankind to follow, primarily to guarantee every person's success in relationships such as marriage, parenting, business, government, church affiliation, or organizations. He did this to make it possible for all humankind to be included in the application and spiritual-employment process of representing His company in all areas of human life. His desire for our success derives from His loving and dynamic nature.

However, due to Satan's influence (greed, cheating, jealousy, competitiveness, etc.) upon humankind, the original plan that the Founder designed for the success of all relationships and institutions has been tainted by sin. This tainting has led to the collapse of many well-intended relationships, which were once solid as a rock. Nonetheless, the Founder continues to show his endless love, grace, and mercy to the just and the unjust in an effort to allow ample time for the unjust to repent and turn away from their evil ways of destroying their personal and business relationships before it is everlasting too late.

For those who obey his company policies, which are written in the Handbook, their rewards for faithfulness are endless. But for those who choose not to follow company policies, the consequences will have an eternal verdict in hell. The Founder has not made the rules for success impossible for us to follow. Quite the contrary, a simple choice to do right or do wrong is what He gently offers. He does not force anyone to do either.

Making the right choices and having godly motives—obeying the standards that the Founder established for you to apply and obtain spiritual employment into His company—can lead to an abundant life of physical, mental, emotional, financial, and spiritual blessings for you and those who you win to Christ. Which will you choose? Apply today—*all* applicants will be accepted!

> *The steps of a good man are ordered by the Lord: and He delights in his way. Though he falls, he shall not be utterly cast down: for the Lord upholds him with His hands.*

—Psalm 37:23–24 (NKJV)

# Chapter 5

## Introduction to Orientation and Training

Congratulations on your new spiritual employment status with the Founder's company! On behalf of the Founder, CEO, and GM, we welcome you to orientation and training class, which will take place from chapter 5 through the end of chapter 20.

By now, you should know who, what, when, where, why, and how the Founder's company was created. Also, now that you are saved, you should know that God's purpose for your life is for you to take the gospel and share it everywhere you go to win lost souls to Christ. But first, you must attend orientation and training class in order to learn how to apply His Word in your own life as well as to teach others the Good News.

Your orientation and training will provide you all the right tools you need to become successful in the Founder's company. There is no such thing as "fake it 'til you make it" with this company. You simply cannot get away with it because the Founder knows you quite well. He knows every hair on your head, and He knows the true desires of your heart (read Luke 12:7; Psalm 37:4).

The Founder created the employment process for on-the-job training in His company and job placement throughout the world so that you, His employee, would become knowledgeable about His company and the spiritual world in and around you. He designed the Handbook to answer every type of on-the-job scenario that you would ever encounter. During this training session, you will learn in detail the characteristics and principles of working for the Founder. You will also learn how the company is secured and how you, as an employee, have access to the company's security systems.

Furthermore, the orientation handbook includes explanations, specific scriptures, and illustrations on topics such as character, the purpose of spiritual gifts, honor, respect, commitment, the elevation of mind (spiritual nutrition), faith (spiritual currency), motivation on the job, teamwork, dressing for success, employee evaluation, promotion, continuing education, job security and benefits, retirement, and termination. Now let's turn to the next chapter and learn the Bible as it relates to the Ten Commandments.

*How much better to get wisdom than gold! To get understanding is to be chosen rather than silver.*

—Proverbs 16:16

# Chapter 6

## BIBLE (Basic Instructions Before Leaving Earth)

We all go through uncomfortable situations in life, and we'll continue to experience trials as long as we are in this fleshly body. But how we behave and handle our storms while we're going through them will determine the outcome of our lives. It is in the latter stage of character development that a person learns to apply the A, B, C's—Always Be Christlike. The Handbook is the best source of help for new and seasoned employees of the Founder to develop godly character while enduring tests, trials, and temptations. When you read and meditate on God's Word, it will, in turn, keep you safe in God's will.

**Character**

In training new employees of the Founder, the first topic that we must address deals with character: how should we behave toward one another as new or seasoned disciples for Christ? Two scripture references come to mind in answering this important question. The first one is universally well-known as the golden rule, or principle of reciprocity, found in Matthew 7:12 (NIV):

> So in everything, do to others what you would have them do to you, for this sums up the Law and the Prophets.

Then, in Mark 12:30–31 (ESV), it is written (emphasis added),

> Love the Lord your God with *all* your heart and with all your soul and with *all* your mind and with *all* your strength. The second is this: "Love your neighbor as yourself." There is no commandment greater than these.

If all employees would take these two scriptures to heart, there would be no need to devise a Handbook such as the Bible. If every employee walked in love toward God and one another, then there would be no jealousy, envy, racial discrimination, bigotry, division, conflicts, wars, pandemics, divorces, greed, poverty, church and business splits, and so forth. Sure, these types of injustices would remain in the world but not among us, the Founder God's employees. But sadly, that's not the case.

Thus, we have to abide by written laws or commandments to maintain peace, unity, order, and brotherly love and produce fruit for the kingdom of God. So, the first thing we must do is make it a habit to love and treat one another with care and concern, and then other areas of our lives will flow properly. It's really not that hard; you just have to follow through on developing some key character traits.

Jesus's life on earth was the personification of the proper character to know and emulate. His life was difficult, yet He treated others with the same degree of love and care that He desired for Himself. Like water flowing freely in a stream, His character illuminated with the fruit of the Spirit—love, joy, peace, longsuffering, kindness, goodness, faithfulness, gentleness, and self-control (read Galatians 5:22–23). Being exemplary of moral excellence, Jesus became the perfect model for everybody, especially employees of the Founder, to aspire to be like.

In 2 Peter 1:5–7 (NKJV), we are provided with a daily plan to assist us in manifesting the character of Jesus:

> Add to your faith, virtue, to virtue, knowledge, to knowledge, self-control, to self-control, perseverance, to perseverance, godliness, to godliness, brotherly kindness, and to brotherly kindness, love.

## The Ten Commandments

One of the first and especially important company policies listed in the Handbook is the Ten Commandments. These commandments are quite simple, practical, and easy to understand; but since the fall of Adam and Eve, throughout history, it has been difficult for humans—in their carnal state of mind—to steadily practice. The effects of disobedience have shown that the impact can be extremely harmful and destructive to ourselves and our relationships with one another. It could ultimately wipe out humankind from the face of the earth. This is because all the items on the list are pathways in which Satan can work his evil plots through you when you break just *one* commandment. According to James 2:10 (KJV),

> For whoever keeps the whole law and yet stumbles at just one point is guilty of breaking all of it.

For example, if you cannot love God and your neighbor as yourself, then you will be unable to follow the Founder's commandments. This is because "love is the fulfilling of the law" (read Romans 13:10). Love is the key ingredient that compels people to want to do what is morally right. On the other hand, if obeyed, they can prevent you from many heartaches and pains in life. By obeying this list, you can receive the benefits and retirement plan that the Founder's company has to offer you. All the policies and examples provided in the Handbook are important for you to know and understand.

---

**Love is the key ingredient that compels people to want to do what is morally right.**

---

Subsequently, the Founder, in His infinite wisdom, has provided multiple safeguards for us to obey and live by through the Ten Commandments to rid ourselves of and avoid acting on "sins that may arise in the heart and mind" (read Matthew 5:19–20). The Ten Commandments that Moses wrote to God's employees are clearly listed in Exodus 20:1–17 (NKJV) as follows:

- You can have no other god or master but the Founder.

If you choose to place anyone else above God, this will lead to your swift termination in the company. This includes moonlighting with fraternities, sororities, the Masonic order, or any occult group or person that tries to defame the name of God by putting their organization and their work in the public's eye and not acknowledging God first. You are never off the clock when you serve the Founder. Therefore, "No one can [temporarily or occasionally] serve two masters; for either he will hate the one and love the other, or else he will be loyal to the one and despise the other" (Matthew 6:24 NKJV). Once you are employed with the company, you are a full-time employee for the Founder. Therefore, you absolutely cannot love anything or anyone *more than* you love God. There is only one Love that is greater than all, and His name is *Yah* (God).

- You cannot make anything for yourself that is a graven or carved image of any type.

This includes anything that resembles what is in heaven above, the earth below, or in the water under the earth. This includes symbols of status such as prime land, houses, luxury cars, tattoos, animals, lakefront properties, etc. You cannot bow down to or serve them, for the Founder has said in Exodus 20:4–5, "You shall [*not*] worship them or serve them; for I, the Lord thy God, am a jealous God, punishing the children for the sin of the fathers to the third and fourth generation of those who hate me."

When people make things, such as their highfalutin social clubs more important than they really are, God comprehends this action as hatred toward Him or idol worship. Just imagine your spouse loving someone else or something else more than he or she loves you. That mental image doesn't sit well in your heart or mind, does it? Well, that's why God said not to make any person or thing a graven image because this causes problems with your special fellowship with Him as your Creator, as well as your special union with your spouse. Never forget that the Founder does not take kindly to you placing any other form of employment (e.g., idols, graven or carved images) before Him.

Remember this: you did not evolve by your own works but by God's infallible love for you and me, which is why He created us in His image. You were *not* formed of a graven or worldly image but by God's image, which is Spirit and truth! Hence, no one has the right to boast of him or herself or of anything that he or she has accomplished or possessions that he or she has attained. The Bible clearly states in Ephesians 2:9–10 (ESV; emphasis added),

> Not as a result of [humankind's] works, so that no one may boast. For we are His workmanship, created in Christ Jesus for good works, which God prepared beforehand so that we would walk in them.

God created you and me to be His skilled masterful works of art for the purpose of giving praise and glory to His name—which are not a result of our own doing, of humankind's doing, and certainly not of things!

- You cannot by any means slander or make false accusations against the Founder's name.

This simply means that you cannot be on the job misrepresenting Him or the company in any way. God expects His employees to testify of His goodness and faithfulness at all times. He is a good, good Father, and deserves to be glorified, honored, and praised for filling your life with good things!

- You must remember to keep the Sabbath day holy.

This is the day that the Founder has set for rest. The Founder, being an extremely hard worker Himself, requires that all His employees work six days a week and rest on the seventh day. (This is because in six days, the Founder made the heavens and earth, and He rested on the seventh day.) The Founder always wants to maintain uniformity for everyone in His company. This means that you should take time to attend church and fellowship with other believers (online or in person), spend quality time with your family, and get proper bodily rest.

- As an employee of the Founder, you must honor your father and your mother on earth.

The Founder is a real family-oriented Boss. His plan for the family is that relationships remain healthy and strong for a lifetime. As an employee of the Founder, your family is a subsidiary of His family. Therefore, He places high regard on the earthly family structure. The chain of command within an earthly family—father, mother, then children—is a part of His nature and design. We can better understand and follow the Founder's guidelines for us when we are within the correct family alignment. In honoring your father and mother, you are honoring the Founder and His plan for your family. This is confirmed in Ephesians 6:2–3 (NKJV), which states:

> Honor your father and mother, which is the first commandment with promise: that it may be well with you and you may live long on the earth.

- You cannot ever deliberately kill or take someone's life.

This act is *never* tolerated by the Founder. This includes premeditated murders such as abortions, homicides, suicides, genocides, euthanasia (mercy killing), and the like. Christ died on the cross praying. He died without any assistance, and humankind should follow His example. According to John 10:18 (NLT) Jesus said, "No one can take my life from me. I sacrifice it voluntarily. For I have the authority to lay it down when I want to and also to take it up again. For this is what my Father has commanded." Based on this scripture, this direct order from the Founder is without exception, and it is clearly stated in the Handbook.

- You cannot by any means commit adultery.

This means if you are married, you cannot have sex with a person other than your spouse. Otherwise, you would be committing adultery. If you are single, then you are not to have sex with anyone. Fornication falls under this category. Even if you are engaged to be married, you are not supposed to have sex until you have committed to each other in holy matrimony unto the Founder. Otherwise, you would be committing premarital sex, which is forbidden by the Founder. Besides, most unmarried adults who live together never make it down the altar and those who do have lower levels of relationship satisfaction and trust.

It is important to note that "looking" at a woman in a lustful manner is considered adultery or fornication (read Matthew 5:28). This is also the case if you look at a man, child, and even pornography. Also, God created and ordained marriage as a sacred union between a man and a woman, which is also the case when dating someone—it should be with the opposite sex (read Genesis 2:24). God's divine design is for man and woman to be suitable companions.

Also, one should be equally yoked with believers in Christ (read 2 Corinthians 6:14). Yes, we are to be friendly and minister to unbelievers to provide them with biblical truths and win them to Christ, but to develop close relationships (temporarily or permanently) is not advocated by God because that could cause us to compromise our biblical values and endanger our stable Christian witness if we are not careful. According to James 4:4 (KJV), "the world, in all its corruptness, hates God and godliness."

Every time a Christian, whether he or she is single or married, closely intermingles with worldly people—they fall into fornication, adultery, distrust, dishonesty, or other unstable and confusing situations. Just as the old saying goes, "Oil and water don't mix." The same is true that neither same-sex couples nor believers with unbelievers mix well. Moreover, those who try to change their sexual gender to conform to biblical principles are *still* in rebellion against God's purpose and plan for their life (read Romans 1). God created humankind for His glory, not our own. Hence, there are no alternatives to this commandment.

- You cannot, at any time, steal or take anything that is not yours, which you haven't been given permission to have.

God placed Adam in the garden to work; therefore, stealing is considered a crime. Work is good for you because it brings income so you can support yourself and your family. In other words, work is your friend; your enemy is laziness because it leads to poverty.

- You cannot, at any time, bear false witness against or lie to your neighbor.

An example of this would be falsely accusing someone of robbing your home when, in fact, you have no witnesses or proof that it happened. Even the legal system has laws stating that a witness must be present to prosecute a defendant. In the court of law, you cannot convict a person based on hearsay.

- You cannot covet or desire to have things that belong to someone else.

This includes a person's spouse or any of their property. When you obey this commandment, you free yourself from giving into lust, jealousy, envy, greed, and other temptations, which are pathways for Satan to lure you to break it and any other commandment that the Founder has ordered you not to do.

The Founder has firmly established these ten rules, which are known as the Ten Commandments in order to bring great rewards into the lives of His obedient employees. These commandments apply to all humankind—both male and female. Furthermore, the Founder lovingly placed these commandments for us to follow so that we would not fall prey to the destructive attacks devised against us by Satan. These commandments were not put in place to hurt, harm, reject, neglect, or stifle anyone or a particular group of people. But God designed them for our lives to have order, balance, and righteous (healthy) boundaries so that *all* who follow Him would enjoy life together and get along with one another here on earth rather than experience separation and division due to conflicting opinions.

For some of you reading this book, to say you know God yet deliberately choose to disobey His commandments is to lie regarding your salvation. Truth is; you cannot possibly know or love God if you despise any of His commandments. For the Bible explicitly says in 1 John 2:4 (NKJV) that "he who says, 'I know Him,' and does *not* keep His commandments, is a liar, and the truth is *not* in him" (emphasis added).

Also, it is important to note that if you willfully choose to disobey any of these commandments, you will be in jeopardy of termination from the Founder's company. This means that if you die a lost sinner (that is, without repenting of and turning away from your sins), instead of going to heaven, God said that your eternal home would be in *hell*. The Bible clearly states in 1 Corinthians 6:9–11 (KJV; emphasis added),

> Do you not know that the *unrighteous* will not inherit the kingdom of God? Do *not* be deceived: neither the sexually immoral, nor idolaters, nor adulterers, nor men who practice homosexuality, nor thieves, nor the greedy, nor drunkards, nor revilers, nor swindlers will inherit the kingdom of God. And such were some of you. But you were washed, you were sanctified, you were justified in the name of the Lord Jesus Christ and by the Spirit of our God.

Some of you reading this book may ask, why would a good, loving, kind, and forgiving God send people to hell? However, you must keep in mind that God doesn't want to send anyone to hell. But if a person decides to disobey and rebel against biblical principles and His commandments (after coming into the knowledge of the truth), then he or she will reap the consequences of their thoughts, words, and actions. Remember what I mentioned in the beginning of chapter 2: God is sovereign and just. Because He created us, He knows what is right for all His creation. Our responsibility is to follow God's will, not try to make Him accept ours.

As you read the Bible, you will discover that these are the same commandments that were given to Moses and His people as they fled from Egypt. The laws have not changed over the years, and thus, they apply to us today. If you break one of these commandments, you *will* fall prey to the wiles of Satan. Don't fool yourself; Satan uses your weaknesses to ensnare you. Once he's got you into sin, he will take you further than you ever wanted to go, and it will take you longer than you ever wanted to stay. Satan doesn't play fair; he's a lowdown, dirty dog!

> **Our responsibility is to follow God's will,
> not try to make Him accept ours.**

Many employees of the Founder have broken some of these commandments. Perhaps you may have broken some of them in your past, and others will break at least one of these commandments in the future during their walk with the Founder. The Founder was well aware, before you were ever born, of your tendency to fall short of obeying His commandments. That's why He is full of love and mercy, pulling you back into His will for your life. He has put into place provisions to assist His employees when they find themselves tempted or have actually broken a commandment. Be careful not to abuse the grace of God by continuing in your sins because you never know when your life will end. Tomorrow isn't promised to anyone.

## The Holy Spirit

Although the Founder does not always remove the consequences from our lives, it is refreshing to know that we have immediate access to Him through Jesus, the CEO, and the Holy Spirit, the GM, in order to get us back on track in His will. It is through the CEO that we are able to communicate with the GM, who assists us in minimizing the damage caused by breaking a commandment. But we must first call upon the CEO and sincerely seek forgiveness, restoration, and reconciliation when asking for His assistance anytime we have violated one of the Founder's commandments.

The GM then acts as a liaison on your behalf and intercedes (directly to the Founder) for you. You see, the GM is like a negotiator for you. This is why it is important to pay attention and listen to Him. He is always at work for you, eagerly working hard to keep you in alignment (or in right standing) with the Founder. And He communicates with you on your level of understanding. He is your guide, and He is part of the Founder's chain of command, which is the trinity—the Father, the Son, and the Holy Spirit.

As you begin to seek the truth regarding *any* situation in your life, you will find that the Holy Spirit will provide you with answers *directly* from God. So wait on His answers and follow His directives for your life. The Holy Spirit is your very own GPS to the Founder: God's Plan of Salvation—for you!

> *Whoso despiseth the Word shall be destroyed: but he that feareth the commandment shall be rewarded.*

—Proverbs 13:13 (KJV)

# Chapter 7

## Purpose of Spiritual Gifts

Every person who comes on board with the company is graciously bestowed with spiritual gifts by the Founder. You have at least one gift inside you. It is this gift that will enable you to find real fulfillment and purpose to continue the mission of the CEO. Although pastors/priests, prophets, apostles, teachers and evangelists are on the cutting edge of demonstrating their spiritual gifts as leaders, they also need the body of believers to help carry out a host of auxiliary duties (ministry of help and support), in the church and marketplace. For example, there are those who use their gifts to usher, sing, pray, and perform outreach services to troubled youth, single parents, prisoners, alcohol and drug addicts, the homeless, the elderly, and so on, so the entire body of Christ has good and perfect gifts that come from the Founder. The Handbook teaches us this fact in James 1:17 (KJV):

> Every good gift and every perfect gift is from above, and comes down from the Father of lights, with whom there is no variation or shadow of turning.

Also, in Romans 11:29 (NKJV), it affirms this:

For the gifts and the calling of God are irrevocable.

## The Purpose of Spiritual Gifts

When the Founder started the company, He wanted to make sure that all who worked for Him understood their purpose. The Founder created the Handbook and filled it with a vision in mind just for you to carry out. He also provided a piece of Himself inside each of you with the hope that you would use your gift for the purpose of furthering His company's mission.

With that purpose comes a plan or goal to achieve whatever God created you to accomplish. When you have a purpose, you make an *intentional* decision to seek to accomplish something you desire. The purpose that was taught by the many experienced employees of old is to always keep our eyes fixed on doing all that we can for the Founder's company so that we will receive our full reward when we retire from our earthly duties.

Gifts are not given merely for the sake of possessing, hoarding, naming, or boasting about them. There is significant meaning behind God's idea for providing us with gifts. The main reason is this: God uses spiritual gifts to be given away to help solve issues within the body of Christ. In other words, the purpose of these gifts is for each employee to use them in service for the mission of the company—first to lead others to salvation and then minister healing, deliverance, and reconciliation to broken lives, including broken vessels, within the body of Christ. Moreover, gifts are given to employees of the Founder for the purpose of edifying (teaching), exhorting (comforting and encouraging), and strengthening (building up) one another in faith.

---

**God uses spiritual gifts to be given away to help solve issues within the body of Christ.**

---

The gifts are as varied as the purposes and plans the Founder has for each of His employees. This means that the Founder saw fit to distribute spiritual gifts among the body of Christ based on the grace He has given to each of us. For example, some of us have been given the gift of contributing (e.g., monetary or material things). Some of us have been given the gift of giving aid (e.g., presiding over or assisting with missions/outreach ministries), which is considered a marketplace ministry or "a church without walls." And some of us have been given the gift of providing mercy to those who just need another chance to correct their wrongdoings (e.g., judges, counselors, managers, teachers, spouses, parents, and other authority figures). The wonderful message here is that *all* believers have been called to practice these gifts; some more frequently and heartily than others according to the measure of grace, faith, and abilities the Founder has given each individual. Romans 12:6–8 (KJV) speaks of these gifts as follows:

> Having then gifts differing according to the grace that is given to us, let us use them: if prophecy, let us prophesy in proportion to our faith; or ministry, let us use it in our ministering; he who teaches, in teaching; he who exhorts, in exhortation; he who gives, with liberality; he who leads, with diligence; he who shows mercy, with cheerfulness.

This scriptural reference is saying that if you have a gift to teach, counsel, minister, worship, sing, praise, dance, preach, show mercy, give money, and so on, then use it in proportion to your faith! The gift that you're sitting on is loaded with potential. It is your key to success. Through exercising your gift, others will be blessed and some of you will even reap financial rewards. Proverbs 18:16 (NKJV) makes this powerful declaration:

> A man's gift makes room for him, and brings him before great men.

Go forth and plant yourself in a ministry or outreach that will make room for *your* gifts. Remember that your gift extends beyond the walls of the church building. In other words, you are a church without walls!

## Holy Spirit

It is important to remember that the one who gives the employees of the Founder the power to execute their gifts is the Holy Spirit. Through the power of the Holy Spirit, an employee of God can express his or her faith successfully either by word or deed. Since spiritual gifts are executed by the third person of the Godhead, no one can boast that he or she earns or deserves them because they are freely given. The Bible declares in 1 Corinthians 1:29–31 (KJV),

> That no flesh should glory in his presence. But of Him are ye in Christ Jesus, who is made unto us wisdom, and righteousness, and sanctification, and redemption: That, according as it is written, He that boasts, let him boast in the Lord.

No matter how small your spiritual gift may seem to be, it plays an incredible role in strengthening the faith of others who need grace. There is nothing more pleasing to God than to see us, His employees, using our faith to exercise our gifts so that the world might marvel at Him and say, "Look at God!" When it is all said and done, God will hold us accountable for how we used our gifts to either help the entire church, including the disadvantaged, the fatherless, and the widowed or to live high on the hog to please ourselves.

> *Each of you should use whatever gift you have received to serve others, as faithful stewards of God's grace in its various forms. If anyone speaks, they should do so as one who speaks the very words of God. If anyone serves, they should do so with the strength God provides, so that in all things God may be praised through Jesus Christ. To Him be the glory and the power for ever and ever. Amen.*

—1 Peter 4:10–11 (NIV)

# Chapter 8

## Honor, Respect, and Commitment

In today's society, there are many reasons that a person can receive honor. For example, you can be honored for being a professional athlete, for academically ranking in the top ten of your graduating class, for becoming Miss USA, for retiring after working thirty years for a company, and for many other accomplishments. These aforementioned accomplishments are admirable qualities that deserve to be recognized and rewarded, but if God is not honored or glorified in all that you do—whether in your work, worship, leisure time, or family life, then it is *all* in vain.

Those who are strong, attractive, intelligent, and talented often find it easier to honor, respect, and trust themselves rather than God who gave them their gifts and talents. Some people fail to realize this (until later): if you receive earthly honors and are not living a life that is pleasing to the Founder, it will only be a matter of time for you to hit rock bottom. If you don't believe me, then recall what happened to Elvis

Presley, Len Bias, Marilyn Monroe, Anna Nicole Smith, Tupac Shakur, Notorious B.I.G., Jimmy Hendrix, Brian Jones, Michael Jackson, Whitney Houston, and countless other exceptionally talented athletes, musicians, and entertainers who received worldly honors. Because they didn't honor, respect, or commit themselves to God, their lives tragically ended as a consequence of overdosing on drugs and alcohol or of being gunned down in the streets! "Those who want to get rich fall into temptation and a trap and into [many] foolish and harmful desires that plunge people into ruin and destruction" (1 Timothy 6:9 NIV).

When God is not first in your life, you'll end up last! (According to a recent report from The New York Times, prescription pills rank as the number-one drug use in America today.)

---

**When God is not first in your life, you'll end up last!**

---

Jesus said, "If you live by the sword, you will die by the same sword." (Matthew 26:52 KJV)

What does it profit a man to gain the whole world and lose his soul? (Mark 8:36 KJV)

Thus, you must honor God for what He has done in your life so your trust will not become misplaced, for surely, misplaced trust leads to a downward spiral of destruction.

Throughout Jesus's teachings, as recorded in the Handbook, He taught us to honor the Founder so that our lives would go well here on earth. When we honor the Founder, He blesses us in unbelievable ways that worldly success alone could never compete with or measure up to. Let's always bear in mind that no matter who admires us or whom we may admire—no one can beat God's system of blessings. When we honor God, He makes us shine (throughout our earthly life) before even the greatest of men! A life that brings honor to God is blessed, and without sorrow. According to Proverbs 10:22 (NKJV),

The blessing of the Lord makes one rich, and He adds no sorrow with it.

## What Does It Mean to Honor God?

In honoring God, first, you must understand what the term really means. One definition that is relative to God states that to *honor* means "to hold in high regard or respect, as for worth, merit, or rank." Another definition of honor is "to show high esteem" (but not with pride, for it is an abomination unto the Founder).

When you honor someone, you admire and appreciate them for the meaning and value they bring into your life. In other words, you desire to gain something from them, such as some character traits. Simply put, admiration is nothing more than genuine love and respect shown towards a person who has made a difference in your life. It is the difference makers that change the world!

> **Admiration is nothing more than genuine love and respect shown towards a person who has made a difference in your life.**

## Eight Ways to Honor God

There are eight ways that all employees of the Founder should honor Him. The *first* is by giving your life to Him.

The Bible says in 1 Corinthians 6:20 (NKJV), "For you were bought at a price; therefore glorify God in your body and in your spirit, which are God's." This means your life is no longer your own because Jesus has redeemed you from the bondage of sin, which once enslaved you under Satan's influence. Now that you are an employee of the Founder, He expects you to honor Him by keeping your mind, body, and spirit pure. Your life is considered to be a living sacrifice—holy and pleasing to God, which is your reasonable or spiritual act of worship (Romans 12:1). Hence, it is important that you guard your thoughts, emotions, words, and actions. In your daily life as God's employee, you should exercise righteousness, peace, love, forgiveness, sexual purity, and whatever is good in His sight.

After you have given your life to God, the *second* step you should make in honoring God involves getting to know Him.

When you meet someone new, you have to spend time getting to know them—their background, personality type, the city they grew up in, their interests and hobbies, how many siblings they have, what they like or dislike, and so on. In this same manner, every employee of the Founder must devote time praying, reading the Bible, fellowshipping with other believers, attending church services, praising Him, sharing concerns with Him, and listening to His voice to cultivate a personal and strong relationship with God. This means you must get to know the Founder in His authoritative role as well as in His vulnerable state of suffering and dying on the cross. Philippians 3:10 (KJV) confirms,

> That I may know Him and the power of His resurrection, and the fellowship of His sufferings, being made conformable unto His death.

Now that you are an employee of the Founder, your goal is to become like Him in your thoughts, speech, behavior, and lifestyle.

The *third* way that you should honor God is by trusting and obeying His commandments. Proverbs 3:5–6 (NKJV) asserts all employees of the Founder to "trust in the Lord with *all* your heart and lean not to your own understanding, in *all* your ways acknowledge Him and He shall direct your paths" (emphasis added).

There will always be seasons of uncertainty in your life, but the way you find answers to help you get through and overcome challenging times is by putting your trust in the Lord and obeying what He tells you to do. For example, in times when you are low in money, but the bills still have to be paid, you must speak and believe Philippians 4:19 (NKJV), which states, "My God shall supply *all* your need according to His riches in glory by Christ Jesus" (emphasis added).

Believing the scriptures is being practical because what you are saying is this: "although I don't know how this bill is going to get paid, but, God, you have the wisdom and the resources to do it, and you promised that you will make a way for me when I'm insufficient to meet my own needs." The cause of your need may be due to an illness that has prevented you from working a job, or perhaps you are a divorced single parent and you've lost the income from the spouse who has abandoned the marriage. Whatever the case may be, God will provide the wisdom and the financial help you need to overcome any problem you face in life. Your job is to trust Him wholeheartedly and obey His instructions!

The *fourth* way that you should honor God is by giving the first tenth of your income to Him (by giving to the local church body where you regularly attend or an outreach ministry such as a local city rescue mission). Although God doesn't need your money, He asks for the first part of your increase so you will always remember to put Him first in all that you do. By giving your first tenth, you are honoring God and helping the church or outreach ministry remain an active voice in your community. You're helping to meet the needs of the poor and the needy. You're learning how to manage the rest of the 90 percent leftover while allowing God to bless you even the more! Proverbs 3:9–10 (NLT) says,

> Honor the Lord with your wealth and with the best part of everything you produce. Then He will fill your barns with grain, and your vats will overflow with good wine.

The *fifth* way that you should honor God is by committing everything you do (in prayer and works) to Him. It is easier to commit big projects, problems, or goals that we want to accomplish into God's hands, but it is tempting to leave Him out of little things that we think we can handle without Him. For example, you routinely take your trash to the dumpster nearest your neighborhood, but God tells you to wait or go to another dumpster. You're thinking, *I'll just do what I've been doing*, and on your way to the dumpster, you find that traffic has been detoured because the police found a dead body lying near the dumpster that you routinely utilize. This is what happens to people when they don't commit every part of their lives to prayer.

Now let's look at a different example to see what the outcome is if you commit your plans to God in prayer. You and your spouse have been trying to get pregnant for five years, and since it hasn't happened yet, you think that it is not the will of God for you to have your own children. (At times, that is the case for some people, but not for you.) Until now, all you've done is complain and drive back and forth to the doctor's office to see what he thinks about your situation. You haven't completely committed the issue to God. Well, finally, a lightbulb goes off in your spiritual mind. By faith, you decide to commit your barren issue to God in prayer, and a year later, you discover that you're pregnant with twins! The Bible tells us in Proverbs 26:3, "Commit [or trust] to the Lord whatever [activities] you want to do, and your plans will succeed." When you commit everything to God in prayer and you work your plan, you shall succeed!

The *sixth* way that you should honor God is by honoring and respecting His principles and those whom He has placed in authority over you. This includes your parents, teachers, employers, landlords, police officers, and spiritual leaders in the church body. The Founder established authority to keep order in the earth. The only time you should break a law is when it goes against God's principles. For example, if you are single and the laws of the land permit you to cohabitate with your girlfriend or boyfriend, then you should check out your all-inclusive Handbook to see what God says about the matter.

> **The only time you should break a law is when it goes against God's principles.**

God does not respect fornication because there is no genuine love, trust, honor, respect, or commitment in shacking up—it leaves too much room for the two people involved to play house, make babies, then pack up and abandon the relationship at any time. This type of nonchalant open relationship only leads to guilt, shame, hurt, disappointment, and condemnation. When the relationship is all over, other people are affected: kids, grandparents, other relatives, and friends of the family. The loss causes emotional, relational, and financial consequences, not between just the couple but others involved in their lives. If this type of shacking up continues without correction, it can also lead a person to hell!

God sees those who are crippled by a lifestyle of fornication or adultery, and He is *calling* the wounded teens, men, and women caught up in this vicious cycle. He is calling you out of this type of lifestyle so that you will walk toward a righteous, happy, and rewarding life through Jesus Christ. If you are in a situation of this kind—whether a heterosexual or homosexual cohabiting state—out of honor and respect to God, you should humbly submit yourself to a trustworthy biblical or pastoral counselor who can assist you in overcoming your fears, doubts, emotional wounds, and losses so you can get on the road to recovery.

Just as Jesus took the woman with the issue of blood who had been tattered, He will take your life and change it too and make you honorable and fit to do great things in life. But to be blessed by God, Hebrews 13:17 (KJV) admonishes all employees of the Founder to,

> Obey them that have the rule over you, and submit yourselves: for they watch for your souls, as they must give account, that they may do it with joy, and not with grief: for that is unprofitable for you.

The *seventh* way you should honor God is by respecting or giving His name credit *above* everything and every name. God gave us Jesus, and at the mention of His name, every knee shall bow in heaven and earth, and every tongue shall confess that He is Lord! (Philippians 2:9–11) So when we lift His name on high above men, degrees, money, material things, and even *unfavorable* circumstances—it pleases God.

For example, in 2007, my wife was diagnosed with metastatic breast cancer fifteen months after she gave birth to Sara. (Metastatic breast cancer is the worst of its kind because it typically spreads to the bones, regional lymph nodes, brain, liver, and lungs.) During this time, she was formerly married, but she had to undergo cancer treatment alone (she barely knew anyone in the new city where the ex-husband moved them). This meant that she had to give up her salaried job and place little Sara with a Christian couple (whom she only met twice) to care for her needs until God saw Victoria through her battle with cancer.

On several occasions during the cancer treatments, Victoria's cells fell below one thousand counts. One night, she ended up in the emergency room with a fever above 103 degrees, chills, profuse sweating, and a dangerously low cell count. During this time, the doctor calmly and firmly said to my wife's former mother-in-law, "She's seriously in trouble, and her condition could possibly be fatal. She may not make it through the night." My wife heard this too and immediately burst out with a song of praise unto God. She started singing,

> As the deer panteth for the waters so my soul longeth after thee. You *alone* are my heart's desire and I long to worship You. You *alone* are my strength, my shield; for You *alone* doeth my Spirit yield. You *alone* are my heart's desire and I long to worship You.

Then she said that she cried out to God, saying, "My confidence is only in You, Lord Jesus Christ, whose name is above every name. Therefore, I shall *not* be moved by the doctor's report. You are my Redeemer, and I *must* live to mother little Sara, cause, Lord, she is dependent upon me. Lord, I can't die right now! I trust You, Lord, and I give your name the praise for what you are about to do in my situation."

Suddenly the Lord came in, and within a day and a half of being hospitalized, He increased her cell count from only 700 blood counts to 14,500 blood counts! Then her oncologist excitedly said, "Somebody upstairs"—pointing her index finger toward heaven—"is taking good care of you because this is nothing short of a miracle! I didn't do it for you! I couldn't have done this for you! Even if I could have done anything to help you, it would have taken at least three weeks to do, and you still would only have about 2,500 cells. But your cell count went through the roof within a day and a half of your emergency hospitalization. That's miraculous! You can pack up and go home now!" The doctor walked out of the room, shaking her head and smiling in amazement! The Bible says in Proverbs 18:14 (NKJV), "The Spirit of a man will sustain him in sickness, But who can bear a broken spirit?"

Everybody doesn't always come through a life-threatening illness victoriously like my wife did, especially when they are forsaken and left for dead! But everything—whether good or bad, happy or sad—happens under God's sovereign will. God knows the end from the beginning, and He will do His good pleasure (read Isaiah 46:10). Thus, man can do nothing without God's permissive will.

After two years of fasting and praying, Victoria had to give up the desire to be married to focus on God's will for her to live (be cancer free) and be a mother to little Sara. At times, she felt vulnerable, afraid, and lonely because this was a hard road to travel, especially with only the support of complete strangers. She didn't like the fact that her marriage was ending during the time of her illness. But God doesn't ask us to like or to defend man's ways but to have faith in Him. Regardless of what man does to you, put your trust in God. I encourage you to keep this in mind the next time you or someone you love is facing a divorce or other trials that don't go your or their way.

> **God doesn't ask us to like man's ways or to defend them but to have faith in Him.**

Whether a marriage is restored, or God allows it to end—He still works a miracle of restoration in the innocent person's life. Whether a person is healed, or God takes them home to be with Him—He still works a miracle to get them out of the pain in their body. God knows what is best for all of us. The Bible says in 2 Corinthians 5:8 (NKJV), "to be absent from the body is to be present with the Lord." So honoring His name—above every person, thing, or situation—helps disciple others who may not yet know Him. In my wife's case, she was discipling or making a believer out of her doctors by continuously giving credit to God during her seemingly hopeless situation. In addition to this: God helped Victoria pay off $3.1 million dollars of medical bills because of her faithfulness to him! She's living proof that honoring God pays wonderful dividends! Isaiah 33:6 (BBE) declares,

> And she will have no more fear of change, being full of salvation, wisdom, and knowledge: the fear of the Lord is her wealth.

The *eighth* and final way that you should honor God is by discipling others. God commands all His employees to go and make disciples everywhere they go (Matthew 28:19). This means that if you are a new or a seasoned employee of the Founder, you have the anointing of the Holy Spirit inside you to teach and win others to Christ. After you have become employed with the Founder's company, He gives you the authority (right and power) to tell as many people as possible about His saving grace and how they can live a life of obedience to His Word.

You see, it is an honor for any employee to be chosen by the Founder and His Son, Jesus, to represent Him. It is truly a special occasion for you to be recognized by the Founder and the CEO. It's good to know that when you honor, respect, and commit yourself to the Founder and His Son, Jesus, you will also be honored by Them.

All employees should strive daily to honor, respect, and remain committed to the Father and His Son. Yes, the Founder's standards are high, but His rewards for you are even greater! Jesus led by example so we would have constant instruction on how to live a life that is honorable, respectful, committed, and pleasing to the Founder.

The Founder will never ask you to do anything that He would not do. Nor will He ask you to do anything contrary to His will for your life. He is also loving and just to provide His employees with a means to accomplish every goal that He has set for us. It is refreshing and comforting to experience the love that the Founder has for His employees. We owe Him the utmost respect and honor that only He deserves.

*The fear of the Lord is the instruction of wisdom; and before honor is humility.*

—Proverbs 15:33 (KJV)

# Chapter 9

## Elevation of Mind— Spiritual Nutrition

Since the beginning of time, it has been understood that your actions speak louder than your words. Yes, your actions are a manifestation of your thoughts and define the kind of person you really are. If what is inside your mind is good, then your actions will reflect it. But if what is inside your mind is evil and unhealthy, then your actions will reflect that too. In essence, your thoughts and behavior are one and the same, and so are your responses to how you feel and what you believe. Your mind controls your entire body, and it will determine the direction of your life. Therefore, you should feed it with things that are healthy and mutually beneficial to you and others.

There is an old computer saying that also applies to what you allow into your mind: garbage in, garbage out. For example, your mind needs a healthy diet of information just as your body needs a diet of healthy, nurturing food. If you eat food that is unhealthy—such as those high in fats, cholesterol, sodium, and sugar—your body will not be at its optimum health. With all the unnatural additives that are put in many foods today, millions of people are becoming ill and are dying at an alarming rate from all sorts of illnesses like cancer, heart disease, strokes, and diabetes.

This is why you can't always trust the crops that humankind produces, especially since so many farmers use steroids, pesticides, and other pest-control chemicals to grow and protect their foods. To gain a competitive edge on their competition, many farmers will even lie about how they grow their crops. But when you choose miracle foods—such as green leafy vegetables and fresh fruits, along with lean meats like fish and chicken, which are low in fat and high in proteins—it will help your body function at its peak, and you will feel great!

The same holds true for your mind. It needs to be fed daily with spiritual nutrients that will bear the fruit of the Spirit of God as seen in Galatians 5:22 (NKJV):

> The fruit of the Spirit is love, joy, peace, longsuffering, kindness, goodness, faithfulness, and self-control.

Although we need physical food to sustain our physical lives here on earth, spiritual food holds a far greater value because it teaches us to focus our attention on a lifestyle of godliness rather than on the things of this world, which will eventually pass away. During Jesus's experience on earth, He spent forty days and nights without physical food, but He was never without spiritual food during His tests, trials, and temptations. The point that Jesus made about fasting from food is this: seeking godliness detoxifies a person from thinking about all that this world has or doesn't have to offer.

Natural food can only sustain the physical body, but it cannot bring you spiritual fullness. Only the Founder can provide you with the spiritual satisfaction that your mind, body, and spirit hunger for. That's what spiritual food does; it properly feeds the mind, body, and spirit. It literally fills you with energy to build you up and recharge your faith, hope, and love so that you will remain healthy and strong in your mind, body, and spirit. When your mind is spirit led, you tell your stomach what to eat and when to stop eating because the spirit now has power over the body.

> **When your mind is spirit led, you tell your stomach what to eat and when to stop eating, because the spirit now has power over the body.**

## Four Ways to Develop an Elevated Mind

A successful employee in the Founder's company is one who has an *elevated* state of mind. To develop an elevation of mind, an employee must read the Handbook and do the following:

1. Focus on God, not your problem.
2. Pray about everything.
3. Study the Word to gain wisdom, comfort, and strength.
4. Practice and apply the Word to your life daily.

When you utilize all four of these techniques, your thinking will be transformed and renewed. In Proverbs 23:7 (NKJV), it is written, "For as he thinks in his heart, so is he." What this means is that your thoughts, words, and actions will go in the direction that you allow your mind to take. When your mind is on things that are beneficial for elevation, you will then be more receptive to grow and mature in character as the Founder would have you to become. Building your mind takes a conscious effort to decide that you want to learn about spiritual things, which will penetrate and uplift your thoughts. This is a decision that you must make—no one else can do this for you. Also, there must be a concerted effort on your part in order for you to gain this level of thinking. Frederick Douglass said, "If there is no struggle, there is no progress." Without effort on your part, your thoughts will not improve.

## The Effect of Distractions on the Mind

Sometimes it is not that easy to maintain an elevated mind because of daily distractions that may cause mental and physical fatigue. Distractions come in many forms, such as financial challenges that steal your energy and take you away from your daily dose of mental uplifting. Other examples of distractions are spats with your spouse, crises with your children, distractions from extended family members, friends, or neighbors—all of which can overwhelm you and rob you of your clarity and serenity of thought.

It is during those difficult times that Satan attempts to keep you distracted and discouraged to prevent you from seeking help from the Holy Spirit to overcome these types of trials. Know that Satan has no power over you unless you give it to him! Often, inexperienced employees of the Founder unknowingly give Satan access to them when they allow footholds to enter their lives. This foothold is referenced in the Bible in Ephesians 4:26–29 (NKJV), which states,

> Be angry, and do not sin: do not let the sun go down on your wrath, nor give place to the devil. Let him who stole steal no longer, but rather let him labor, working with his hands what is good, that he may have something to give him who has need. Let no corrupt word proceed out of your mouth, but what is good for necessary edification, that it may impart grace to the hearers.

A foothold for Satan is any thought, word or action—such as stealing, being angry, or speaking condescendingly toward someone—that appeals to the nature of Satan. Thoughts, words, and actions that are contrary to the Founder literally serve as a means of summoning evil and ill will into your life. This is exactly the frame of mind that Satan wants you in so that he can throw distractions in your way to keep you from functioning at your healthiest and most productive level. Reflect back to chapter 2 when I stated that the mission of Satan is to steal, kill, and destroy you; and the best way for him to do that is to manipulate, control, and deceive your mind.

Have you ever noticed how hard it is for a person to focus when he or she has lost control of their thoughts, words, or actions? In any given situation, these types of people tend to become frustrated and argumentative and blame others for the way they behave. When distractions come, they tend to lean toward the negative rather than the positive. That's why it is so critical that you learn how to constantly train your mind to think of things that build you up, not tear you down.

## Six Ways to Maintain an Elevated Mind

Even if you are a negative person today, there is hope to change for a better tomorrow. The first step is to recognize that you have a problem and then be willing to learn how to position yourself mentally, physically, and spiritually for a change. There are different things that you can do to help yourself stay focused.

*First*, make sure that you are in a nonhostile and nonthreatening environment. I know this is a sensitive subject that most people find difficult to discuss, but it needs to be brought to the forefront. If you are being abused by someone either in the workplace or at home, then you should remove yourself from that debilitating and nerve-racking environment and seek safety. There are homeless shelters and battered women and children's shelters that are located in most cities across America if you are needing a safe place to go. Proverbs 24:1–2 (NLT) says, "Don't envy evil people or desire their company. For their hearts plot violence, and their words stir up trouble."

As an employee of the Founder, you cannot afford to be in an environment that is dangerous to you and your children's mental, emotional, physical, spiritual, and financial health and future. So, the best solution is to break away from bad associations and protect yourself and your children first. In this case, it is perfectly okay to put yourself and your children first because your safety is necessary for your survival.

For those already in a safe place, if there are children in your home, take some time aside in your day or evening and go to a quiet place without distractions. (Your spouse, teenagers, parents, or babysitter may assist you with the younger children while you take some *"me"* time or time for yourself.) Also, you can get a few minutes away by taking a brief shower or bath while the kids are sleeping or by singing or listening to a song while preparing a quick meal. It is important to teach your children and other family members to respect your need for brief moments of peace and quiet. As your children are growing up, they will learn how to set aside some time for themselves, as well as allow others to do the same.

*Second*, meditate on scriptures daily. When you meditate, choose scriptures from the Handbook that will inspire and strengthen you simultaneously. Some favorites to learn are the following:

- "I can do all things through Christ who strengthens me" (Philippians 4:13 NKJV).
- "Greater is He that is in me than he that is in the world" (1 John 4:4 KJV).
- "But my God shall supply all your needs according to His riches in glory in Christ Jesus" (Philippians 4:19 KJV).
- "No weapon formed against you shall prosper; and every tongue that accuses you in judgment I will condemn. This is the heritage of the servants of the Lord, and their vindication is from Me, declares the Lord" (Isaiah 54:17 KJV).
- "A thousand shall fall at your side, ten thousand shall fall at your right hand; but it shall not come near you" (Psalm 91:7 NKJV).

When you make these declarations aloud to yourself, make them personal by using first-person (*I*, *me*, and *my*) statements.

You must also consciously say to yourself, "There is nothing that is too big or too small that I can't handle with Christ. Absolutely nothing is bigger than Jesus!" Once you say this and similar affirmations out loud, your mind will subconsciously reflect on the powerful life that is in you and forget the stresses of the day. In meditating, you are offering thanks to the Founder for your blessings, and you are reminding yourself how powerful you are with God, as well as how fragile you are without His Spirit working in and through your life.

---

**Absolutely nothing is bigger than Jesus!**

---

*Third*, keep positive and realistic goals in front of you and work on them a little every day if possible. If you are the main caregiver and you have young children to care for, setting personal goals may be difficult to do depending on their age, especially if you have a preschooler. If that is the case for you, then your current goals should include the needs of your young children, as well as yourself. Your time will come, but the goal of raising healthy children is most important, especially during the first five years of their life. If that is not the case for you, you should get busy writing some definite goals to aim for and then start working toward them on a daily basis. Always consider your strengths when pursuing any goal in life.

*Fourth*, attend a church whose leader teaches sound doctrine, lives a righteous lifestyle, and gives encouraging messages. People come to church with all kinds of problems. With that said, it is important to find a ministry where you can hear positive, inspiring, and life-changing messages that build your faith, hope, and love walk.

*Fifth*, surround yourself with positive people in the faith. Some employees of the Founder think that they can closely associate themselves with both positive and negative people and somehow end up having a positive attitude. This way of thinking is far from the truth! This is even true with math.

With mathematical equations, a negative number plus a positive number equals a negative number if the negative number is larger than the positive. Likewise, in a friendship, if the more dominant person has a negative attitude, he or she will influence the other person to think, speak, and behave negatively. On the other hand, if the dominant person has a positive attitude, he or she will influence the other to think, speak, and behave positively. The point is this: there will always be negative situations and people in your life. But if you think, speak, and behave positively by standing firm on godly principles, you will become a positive-change agent in the lives of those around you.

The *sixth* and final way to elevate your mind is to set it on things that the Founder deems necessary for your spiritual growth. An example of this point is Colossians 3:2 (NKJV): "Set your mind on things above, not on things on the earth." By this, Paul the apostle was teaching us that there are many things that people set their hearts on such as food, money, fine clothes, cars, and houses. Rather than being consumed mentally by those things, we are encouraged to think on the following things found in Philippians 4:8 (KJV):

> Finally, brethren, whatsoever things are true, whatsoever things are honest, whatsoever things are just, whatsoever things are pure, whatsoever things are lovely, whatsoever things are of a good report; if there be any virtue, and if there be any praise, think on these things.

You can strengthen your mind and spirit by studying and meditating often on scriptures like the one above found in the Handbook.

## The Holy Spirit's Influence on the Mind

The Holy Spirit is there with you as a guide to help you understand all that the Founder would have you to know. To create within yourself a clean and untainted mind, you will need to completely allow the Holy Spirit to work in your life. The Holy Spirit works directly with you and enables you to discern right from wrong and good thoughts from bad ones. Listen to the Holy Spirit, who communicates with you through your conscience. The Handbook also warns us in Ephesians 4:30 (NIV):

> And do not grieve the Holy Spirit of God, by whom you were sealed for the day of redemption.

## Putting Off the Old Mind

Many new employees struggle with overcoming old habits that do not bring them closer to the Founder's will and plan for their lives. Know that, all your voluntary actions first originate in your mind; this takes place before you physically carry out any action. This is powerful, and it is also the reason why you have to meditate on the Founder's Word. This is for your benefit and not the Founder's. When you meditate on His Word, you will develop a strong desire to do things the way the Founder has planned and purposed for your life. The Handbook teaches you that when you have committed yourself to being the best employee that you can be for the Founder, *He* is able to change your old ways so that you can become the employee that He desires you to be. Ephesians 4:22–24 (NKJV) tells us:

> that you put off, concerning your former conduct, the old man which grows corrupt according to the deceitful lusts, and be renewed in the spirit of your mind, and that you put on the new man which was created according to God, in true righteousness and holiness.

When you have transformed from doing whatever you want to do to carrying out the will of the Founder, your mind becomes spiritually elevated and renewed! What an awesome mental state to be in! Just imagine the peace and joy that you will have in your life when you can think, speak, and behave like the Founder. In the Handbook, the Founder told King David that "he had a heart after His own" (read Acts 13:22). What a wonderful compliment to receive from the Founder!

When your mind and spirit are elevated, you can have access to the kind of active faith that moves mountains! The process of elevating your mind will require time and discipline in performing all the steps that were outlined in this chapter. While you are developing this state of mind, there will still be occasional tough times. This is simply a part of life. Your mental state of mind will make all the difference as to how you handle those tough times. Your elevated mind will allow you to pull through the storms in life, and you will be mentally stronger when those storms end.

*Let this mind be in you, which was also in Christ Jesus.*

—Philippians 2:5 (KJV)

# Chapter 10

## Faith—Spiritual Currency

Your faith will be tested throughout your lifetime. Therefore, to walk in confidence, you must first develop your faith walk. As you develop your faith, you will be able to endure and triumph over the pressures of life and bear much fruit. The Word of God declares in Romans 10:17 (KJV), "So then faith cometh by hearing, and hearing by the Word of God." In this scripture, the word *hear* means "to receive with a willing and obedient heart." Faith can only be developed through listening and receiving the message of Yahshua the Christ. Once this happens, a person who allows the Holy Spirit to access their heart and mind can exercise faith, which will cause them to rise above any situation and thrust them into greater works for the glory of God.

On the other hand, disobedient employees of the Founder and unbelievers who deprive themselves of hearing the Word of God cannot endure the trials of life and hence block their own blessings. Their unwillingness and disobedience put them in a paralyzed state of mind and prevents them from receiving the faith they need to overcome and rise above their problems. The reason is this:

The natural man does not receive the things of the Spirit of God, for they are foolishness to him; nor can he know them, because they are spiritually discerned. (1 Corinthians 2:14 NKJV)

This says that a person who makes decisions based on his natural senses (what he or she can feel, taste, see, touch, and smell) cannot *hear* (understand) the Founder's ways. This kind of person can only see as far as what is in front of him or her. Thus, they lack the insight to avoid problems, and they lack the faith to perceive and do greater works in life. This is why James 4:2-3 (KJV) says that many who lack faith will "lust for, kill, envy [or covet], fight and war against others who do, yet they cannot have because they ask amiss that they may consume it upon their lusts." Without being willing and obedient to the Word of God, a person will be unable to understand and do all that the Founder calls him or her to do.

Faith is such an awesome expression of your belief and trust in the Founder's promises to you. This is because you can't see it or explain it, yet you *know* beyond a shadow of a doubt that what you believe *will* happen! The Handbook tells us, "Now faith is the substance of things *hoped* for, the evidence of things not seen." (Hebrews 11:1 NKJV; emphasis added). In other words, faith strongly believes that what is hoped for *will* happen before it actually comes to pass.

When God framed the earth, He spoke what He wanted with only His words. Therefore, when you put faith and spoken words together (it must be in alignment with the will of God for your life), your desires will eventually come to fruition.

## Three Things Must Happen for Faith to Work

*First*, you must *believe* that God exists and build a personal relationship with Him. Hebrews 11:6 (NLT) says, "Anyone who wants to come to him *must* believe that God exists" (emphasis added). We know God exists for one simple reason: He pursues us every day to have an intimate relationship with us. That's just the kind of loving and faithful God who created us. He comes to us by way of situations, through the words or deeds of others that prompt our attention to His ways and His miracles. He even comes to us by way of thoughts that come into our mind, which become solutions to difficult and seemingly impossible problems. He uses various methods to grow our faith in Him. According to Psalm 139:1–3 (NKJV), David said (Emphasis added),

> O Lord, You have searched me and known me. You know my sitting down and my rising up; You understand my thoughts afar off. You comprehend my path and my lying down, and are acquainted with *all* my ways.

This scripture informs us that God wants to occupy a special place inside the heart of all His creation. Hence, He really does exist!

*Second*, you must confidently *hope* for what you believe before it comes to pass. It won't happen for you if you are afraid to believe in what you are hoping for. So don't go around with your head hanging down, hoping for something to happen, because your timid behavior will cancel out the faith you need for God to move on your behalf. You must inwardly and outwardly display confident hope in God as you wait for Him to assist you in meeting your expectations. "For the Spirit God gave us does not make us timid, but gives us power, love and self-discipline" (2 Timothy 1:7 NIV).

*Third* and final point: you must sincerely *seek* Him. "He rewards those who sincerely seek him" (Hebrews 11:6 NLT). When you go to God through prayer and petition to seek His help to get you through any situation, then you can expect Him to honor and compensate you. Your actions show that you trust the Founder, and He rewards you when you seek Him first. Proverbs 8:17–18 (KJV) states, "I love those who love me; and those who seek me early shall find me. Riches and honor are with me; yea, durable riches and righteousness."

The best examples of faith are found in the Bible. Many of these employees lived less than perfect lives, but when called upon to join the Founder's team, they leaped in faith at the opportunity. One such employee, found in Joshua chapters 2 and 6, was a young lady named Rahab who lived a lifestyle that was not pleasing to the Founder. Rahab's opportunity to answer the Founder's call arose when she came in contact with two employees of the Founder (one was named Salmon and the other's name is unknown) who were sent to spy on Jericho, the city where she lived. Their plan was to destroy this city and all its inhabitants. This young woman had heard the reports about how fierce the two men were. However, on one night of fate, these men crept into the town where Rahab lived. She was frightened when she saw the men because she thought that they were coming to kill her with the rest of the people of Jericho. Instead, they came to ask her to hide them in her house from the authorities in the city. Rahab knew that her life would be at risk if her people found out that she had assisted these men of God, but she also knew that this would give her an option to save both her and her family. By faith, Rahab *believed* that the spies were protected by the Founder, so she agreed to hide them in her attic.

What makes this story so ironic is that before all this took place, Rahab was a prostitute whose house was strategically located on the wall of the city to easily accommodate travelers to maintain her trade. But after she helped the two men of God, she married one of them, Salmon, and became the mother of Boaz, a wealthy landowner who lived in the town of Bethlehem (a city in the Fertile Crescent). Their marital union put Rahab in the lineage of Jesus and the great-great-grandmother of King David! Rahab's choice was one of faith in God, which led to a turnaround in her lifestyle and tremendous blessings for her future.

You see, the Founder searches the heart of humankind, and He will choose anyone whom He pleases to carry out His plan and purpose. So don't scoff when the Founder calls upon someone whom you might consider less than worthy to serve Him. More importantly, when the Founder calls on you, don't ignore Him because you believe that you're not worthy enough to serve Him. The Founder knows that *all* of us were born into sin. Thus, when He calls on you, He sees something great in you, and He has better plans for your life! So, answer His call! God may call on you directly, or like Rahab, He may catch you off guard and send some of His employees to reach and teach you the right way. Your response to Him will be the most important decision you'll ever make!

### Faith in Action

Faith is the cornerstone of the Founder's company. You must have faith and apply it to receive all that the Founder has in store for you. It has once been said that faith is an action word. This means that faith is more than a thought or a feeling. Faith is belief with action and determination that is so strong that it is manifested into physical existence. When you put the two words together, you get a powerful understanding of faith— *faith action*. Your faith action will cause you to mentally and physically work toward otherwise impossible goals.

Your faith action is the determining factor that can materialize the things you need spiritually, mentally, physically, relationally, and financially. Faith action can heal your mind, body, finances, marriage, and other relationships through meditation and focus on scriptures. Faith is one of the most amazing gifts that you will ever receive from the Founder. It is the *measure* of your faith action that will either allow you to have an intimate relationship with the Founder or hinder it.

> **It is the measure of your faith action that will either allow you to have an intimate relationship with the Founder or hinder it.**

When you put your faith into action, you please the Founder. Without *active* faith, there is absolutely nothing that the Founder can do for you! The Handbook states, "But without faith it is impossible to please Him" (Hebrews 11:6 NKJV). This word *impossible* is a strong testimony from the one who created all things in heaven and on earth. If you truly understand and believe that the Founder is the Creator of all things, would you want to get caught not believing in Him? Well, your faith action is how the Founder measures your belief in and loyalty to Him. It is that simple.

Your faith action is how you put your money where your mouth is, spiritually speaking. Anything else is just lip service. Remember, you cannot fool the Founder. He said in James 2:17 (ESV), "Faith without works is dead," which means your actions must follow your speech and belief.

### Mountain-Moving Faith

It is written in Matthew 17:20 (KJV), "If ye have faith as a grain of mustard seed, ye shall say unto this mountain, remove hence to yonder place; and it shall remove; and nothing shall be impossible unto you." The size of a mustard seed is approximately one-sixteenth of an inch. That is not very much faith at all. But in this parable, it is implied that what is being described is *pure faith*. Pure faith is without any doubt.

An example of this pure faith was once told by an employee from a church pulpit. This employee was a minister who told the story of a small farming town that was in desperate need of rain due to the worst drought ever. Unless they received rain immediately, the town was about to lose all its crops. The preacher of the citizens of this town had called a special prayer service at the church to petition God to send them rain. When the church congregation showed up for the special prayer service, only one of the members came prepared.

Sitting among the unprepared adult church members was a little girl who brought her umbrella. The preacher of this small congregation was touched when he saw the actions of this child. He pointed out to the church that the child was the only one who had enough faith in the power of prayer since she was the only one who brought an umbrella. The story ended with the town receiving rain that day based on the small, pure faith of a child.

Do you have this pure, doubt-free faith of a child? When life's circumstances come to try to steal your joy and peace, you need to step up and present your prayers of faith in the Founder's power to change it. Like the little girl who brought her umbrella to the church prayer service, you need to show up with something as a demonstration of your belief that God will answer the prayers of His people.

There is another story from the Handbook that illustrates pure faith action. In this story, Jesus the CEO saw a severely crippled man who, with much effort, was trying to get into a pool of healing water. Jesus saw the man and asked him, "What are you doing?" The crippled man replied that he wanted to get into the healing water, but others would not permit him to do so. Jesus then asked the man, "Do you want to be healed?"

The man shouted, "Yes!"

Jesus simply said to him, "Take your mat and go." At Jesus's command, the man jumped up and began skipping up and down with joy! Jesus humbly said to the man, "Your faith has healed you. Now go and tell no one who did this. But go to the temple and show the priest."

This true story is a wonderful example of faith action at work. If you notice from the story, the crippled man had to *hear* the Word, then *act* on it by faith! This man had to have the faith of a small mustard seed. He didn't doubt Jesus. Nor did he doubt his own ability to get up and move at Jesus's command. Just imagine what would have happened if this man told Jesus that he couldn't get up or if he had questioned Jesus's word. He wouldn't have ever received his reward of getting up from a stifling situation and confidently walking into a better life. It is worth restating that "for he who comes to God must *believe* that He is, and that He is a *rewarder* of those who diligently seek Him" (Hebrews 11:6 NKJV; emphasis added). As long as you are employed by the Founder, you are to operate in faith—for it is the only way to please the Founder and His Son.

## When Doubt Shows Up

Most people have watered-down faith because they secretly, and often openly, doubt that what they need God to do for them will ever happen. Another popular story found in Matthew chapter 14 tells what happens when we doubt the Founder. This story concerns one of Jesus's closest employees, Peter. He was a fisherman by trade who became one of the twelve disciples of Jesus. (Keep in mind that before the events in this story, Peter had spent quality time with Jesus and personally witnessed many miracles He performed. So, he shouldn't have had any trouble believing in Jesus, right?)

The story unfolds with Peter and the other disciples being in a boat on the Sea of Galilee. Jesus had commanded them to go to the other side of the sea ahead of Him so that he could get alone on the mountainside and pray to the Father. While Peter and the others were on their way to meet Jesus on the other side, a terrible storm had suddenly appeared on the waters. The men feared for their lives as their boat was tossed out of control in the storm. When the disciples saw Jesus walking toward them on the water, their fear increased because they thought He was a ghost.

Knowing their fear, Jesus called out to the men and said, "Take courage, it is I; do not be afraid" (Matthew 14:27 KJV). Peter, in doubt, asked Jesus, "Lord, if it is you, command me to come to you on the water" (Matthew 14:28 KJV). Jesus then instructed Peter, "Come" (Matthew 14:29 KJV). Peter then got out of the boat and began walking on the water toward Jesus. But once Peter felt the strong winds, he became afraid and began to sink. In fear, he called out to Jesus, saying, "Lord, save me!" (Matthew 14:30 KJV). Jesus reached out and caught Peter. Then He said to Peter, "O you of little faith, why did you doubt?" (Matthew 14:31 KJV).

This story ends with Jesus saving Peter and calming the raging storm. All the disciples were safe in Jesus's care, and they proclaimed to Jesus that He was the Son of God! But did these men proclaim in faith, or did they proclaim because of the miracles they had seen Jesus perform? Remember that at the core of faith is "the substance of things hoped for but not yet seen" (Hebrew 11:1 KJV). Faith believes before it sees the physical manifestation!

These two true stories from the Handbook are in sharp contrast to each other. The first story about the crippled man was an example of pure faith in action. In this story, the crippled man was healed because of his complete faith in Jesus. This man had no doubt that Jesus could heal him, and he acted on his faith. In the second story about Peter, it was clear that he lacked faith.

Now, be careful before you throw stones at Peter. Many of us, while reading this story of Peter, would wonder, *How could Peter ever doubt Jesus after seeing all the miracles that He had performed up close and personal?* Imagine what it would have been like for you to have been a close friend of Jesus, as was the case with Peter, and to have had the privilege of listening to all the personal conversations that Jesus so freely shared with Peter and the other disciples concerning truths about the Founder. Surely you are now asking yourself, how could Peter have ever doubted Jesus and lacked faith?

Before you answer that question, recall all the events that you experienced in which you knew Jesus saved you—all the close-call accidents that you almost had and all the impossible tasks that you secretly and openly gave the Founder praises for bringing you through.

We all have had these moments. If you or someone you know hasn't yet experienced a close-call moment, just keep on living.

> **Faith believes before it sees the physical manifestation!**

Now recall those times when you did not go the extra mile, let alone ever attempted the first mile because you lacked faith. Are you sometimes the crippled old man who acted on pure faith? Or do you sometimes doubt like Peter? If we are honest with ourselves, most of us would answer yes to both questions. When you find yourself doubting God, as Peter did, you need to strengthen your relationship with the Founder so your faith in Him will grow and manifest during troublesome times in your life. The Founder promises that "He will never leave nor forsake you" (Hebrews 13:5 KJV). Whenever you feel the emptiness from the absence of God's presence, it is because you are not spending enough time getting to know Him or you have strayed away from Him altogether.

The Handbook is full of many true stories of faithful men and women and the rewards they received for putting their faith in action. The Handbook is also full of just as many true stories about countless men and women who lacked faith, and the consequences they suffered due to doubting the Founder. But many stories also demonstrate the compassion and consistency of the Founder and how He continued to work with and reached out to men and women who doubted Him.

You don't have to learn the hard way like so many before you. You have the Handbook to refer to, as well as weekly (Bible study) training sessions at your local church that can help you stay on track with your faith in the Founder. Be an *active* believer! Remember, you cannot please the Founder without putting your faith into action.

## Faith Is Your Spiritual Currency

Faith is the spiritual currency in the bank of heaven. Once you are employed by the Founder, you are given an open line of credit that can increase as often as you obey His Word and put your faith into action.

Just imagine your account increasing each time you faithfully work within the will of the Founder. Also, imagine there is no limit to how much you can receive from the Founder in blessings, favors, finances, protection, provision, healing, gifts, and peace of mind. No earthly bank account could ever match your account with the Founder because, first, it's spiritual, and then it manifests itself in the physical! Everything that humankind offers you is temporary, whereas the Founder's investment plan for you is holistic and eternal. This is because the finite knowledge of humankind can never compete with the infinite mind of the Founder. "His ways are not your ways; His thoughts are not your thoughts" (Isaiah 55:8 KJV). Your goal as an employee of the Founder is to strive to learn His ways so that you can perform His will.

> **The finite knowledge of humankind can never compete with the infinite mind of the Founder.**

Yes, your faith action makes you one of the wealthiest employees in the company. The Founder does not show any favoritism to anyone, so any employee who chooses to have active faith chooses to please the Founder. And He will reward faith-filled employees with prosperity, not only in dollars and cents. However, the Founder is very practical and knows your needs regarding financial stability to survive in this world. He can provide you with the wisdom that you need to make sound financial decisions if you dare to ask Him. In the Handbook, James, the brother of John and son of Zebedee, said in James 1:5 (NKJV),

> If any one of you lacks wisdom, let him ask of God, who gives to all liberally and without reproach, and it shall be given to him.

Understand this: it is perfectly okay to ask for gifts that would benefit you personally. This is especially true when asking spiritual gifts from the Founder such as wisdom and patience. In 1 Kings 3:1–15, Solomon asked God to give him an understanding heart so that he might righteously judge God's people and discern good from evil.

Because Solomon did not ask for material wealth and worldly power, God honored his request, plus He gave him riches and power.

These are honorable requests because a world evangelist named Daniel Kolenda once said, "You cannot give to others what you do not have." So, if it is more wisdom or patience you personally need, this is a wholesome request, given that as God increases your knowledge and understanding, you can dispense it appropriately to help others, as well as yourself. Remember, though, that your spiritual wealth is dependent upon you physically and mentally working, all the while operating in faith and obedience to the wisdom that the Founder so graciously provides. And yes, discipline to seek the Founder's ways and will is also required of you to arrive at your destination of spiritual wealth. Your expectation, along with spiritual wisdom and discipline, will set the course of your appointed destination.

This loving action of the Founder validates His promise to you: "Seek and you shall find" (Matthew 7:7 KVJ). You will not find your prayer requests honored until you are obedient to the Founder and have properly sought the correct manner to ask and understand the things that you ask of Him.

> **Your expectation, along with spiritual wisdom and discipline, will set the course of your appointed destination.**

This is no different than what one would expect of a child asking his earthly father for something. Just as a child makes a request to his earthly father, you would have to properly make a request to the Founder of something that is beneficial to you before He honors it. And as with the Founder, there are requirements that you must meet before He honors your request, even when you have asked for things that are within His will.

The measure of your faith can literally make or break you. When you are active in your faith, you will receive the Founder's blessings. What a perfect and simple plan for you to have all that you need right at your choosing! And because the Founder's words are true, no one can take this promise away from you, unless you choose to doubt it.

Being active in faith should be a daily habit for every employee of the Founder. Never start your day without faith because the measure of your faith is the measure of your spiritual currency.

## Faith and Works

It is written in the Handbook that "faith without works is dead" (James 2:20 KJV). This means that to please the Founder, you must have faith and works together. In short, you must work your faith! An example of this is found in Genesis chapter 22. It is the famous story of Abraham. When the Founder instructed Abraham to take his only beloved son and sacrifice him on the altar, however strange it seemed, Abraham went to work immediately and followed His command. Through his obedience to the Founder and actively working toward carrying out this shocking command, Abraham clearly put his faith into action. Abraham showed his faith in this act by first being obedient to the Founder and, second, through his belief that the Founder had a perfect plan and reason for this otherwise horrific command. As you may know, this story ends with the Founder faithfully providing a ram in the bush for Abraham to sacrifice in the place of his son, Isaac. What an *awesome* display of faith with works!

If you knew that by faith, you could heal and change situations in your life, wouldn't you practice using it at all times? Faith gives you spiritual strength to do those things that you normally cannot do. Sometimes you may go through a bad time in your life, and it may require that you exercise your faith to get through your issues or circumstances. Every employee should frequently use their faith to overcome trials. The more faith you have, the more confident you are in the Founder's ability to help you.

When every employee in the company exercises faith, it increases the effectiveness of the company. With faith, you can achieve anything good, from the smallest to the greatest of things. Faith is the energy that opens up spiritual doors to the company's corporate office—heaven. It's every employee's desire and dream to finally make it to heaven. To a world-class athlete, heaven is like the Olympics! When you get there, you have won the gold medal!

> **To a world-class athlete, heaven is like the Olympics!**
> **When you get there, you have won the gold medal!**

Before faith manifests itself physically, it is a mental exercise that needs to be practiced often so you don't become rusty on your life's journey. You want your faith to fully operate so you are always ready to use it when challenges arise. For those who have not acted in faith, they find it difficult to understand three things: the importance of active faith, how it works, and how its power brings things into existence. These individuals will either learn how to use it or avoid it altogether.

For any employee who wants to have more faith, you must first learn about it by studying the Handbook, hearing how others overcame, and undergoing various trials throughout your life. The more your faith increases, the closer you will draw to the Founder and Jesus. The ultimate goal of the Father and His Son is to have a relationship with you and to develop a faith within you that can move mountains out of your way! No one in heaven or earth can do the impossible for you like God!

> **The ultimate goal of the Father and His Son is to have a**
> **relationship with you and to develop a faith within you that can**
> **move mountains out of your way!**

Operating in faith doesn't just benefit you as an employee, but it helps build up the employees around you who are new to the company. In the Handbook, it is mentioned that faith is a blessing to those who use it, while a lack of faith will cause those who don't to fall short of their goals. When you step out in faith, you testify that you trust the Founder completely along with His plans for your life. When others see how your faith has helped you overcome and break through barriers, then they will want to go to the Founder too and exercise their faith in situations they will experience during their lifetime.

When you have the faith of a mustard seed, you can move the mountains that come into your life. Sometimes the mountains come in the form of life stressors, such as divorce, trouble on the job or with in-laws, financial issues, challenges concerning your children, sickness, the death of a loved one, or just the everyday burdens of life itself. This is why it requires your faith in the Founder to release you from the power of overwhelming circumstances. It is your faith in God that allows you to be overjoyed about your future and not overwhelmed by your circumstances.

You can never go wrong operating in faith. It is what sets the employees apart from those who don't work for the company. Many try and fake it, but their unbelief has the tendency to show up during the tests and trials of life. You can't pretend in the Founder's business because everything you say and do will be monitored and recorded for your final evaluation. And when the Founder knows that you have faith, then He will grant you honor and rewards.

> **It is your faith in God that allows you to be overjoyed about your future and not overwhelmed by your circumstances.**

The Handbook teaches us that the Founder has given each of us a measure of faith. Therefore, before your faith can grow and before you can receive anything from the Founder, you must first hear and accept His Word. You cannot create faith on your own because it is a gift to you from Him. Once you have heard the Word of God, it is your choice to accept His gift of faith to you and then apply it to every situation you'll encounter to please Him.

*So then faith comes by hearing, and hearing by the word of God.*

—Romans 10:17 (NKJV)

# Chapter 11

## Walking in Confidence

Worldly people brag of themselves, their parents, their children, and their friends when they become wealthy, and influential, acquiring many earthly things, such as luxurious homes, private jets, exotic cars, platinum jewelry, exquisite art, and even some priceless antiques. Self-importance, self-image, and self-confidence are the controlling factors among those who are proud of all their accomplishments and material possessions. They put their confidence and security in the wrong things and inevitably become spiritually, emotionally, physically, relationally, and financially bankrupt.

People who tend to put their confidence in things fail to realize that it can be suddenly taken away through such events as theft, failed marriages and business partnerships, job loss, lawsuits, serious illnesses, and natural elements like fire, hail, water (flood), wind (tornado or hurricane), rust, and moths. In Matthew 6:19–21 (KJV), Jesus said,

> Do not lay up for yourselves treasures on earth, where moth and rust destroy and where thieves break in and steal; but lay up for yourselves

treasures in heaven, where neither moth nor rust destroys and where thieves do not break in and steal. For where your treasure is, there your heart will be also.

Quite the reverse: people who put their confidence in God can walk with the assurance of *knowing* that what they receive from the Founder has a spiritual security system that cannot be ruined by the earth's elements, sickness, foul play, or by a pandemic or a relationship that goes bad. Knowing that the Founder has such protection for the things that He gives you as His employee should make you feel very safe and confident.

The Founder knows how important it is for His employees to be confident and secure in their employment in His company. He also knows that His employees will come across many nonemployees or carnal-minded Christians who will have convincing ideas about life that are contrary to His ways. Furthermore, He knows how difficult it is for you to stand up against opposition when you find yourself in uncertain circumstances that seem beyond your control.

In this chapter, you will be provided an example of moral corruption exuding itself as confidence and examples of how to walk in the confidence of God. You will also learn what it means to have the God kind of confidence, how He sees you, and the benefits of living in confidence with Him.

## What It Means to Have Confidence in God

When people talk about confidence, the word that usually comes to mind is *self-confidence* or *self-worth*. The world's view of self-confidence is that only the fittest survive, which was an idea originated in 1851 by Herbert Spencer. Some evolution theorists, such as Charles Darwin and Spencer, argued about the meaning of the term fittest from an economic, biological, and racial perspective, which caused much confusion about its original meaning. Contrarily, as followers of the Founder God our focus is not on self-anything—whether it be looks, physical fitness, race, reproductive rate, intelligence, social class, educational status, or economic status as a means of survival; rather, we focus on the God kind of confidence, which has the power to ride roughshod over *any* situation! It is God alone that gives us the confidence to do *anything* He has purposed for us to do in life!

If God can prove through a little shepherd boy named David that, against all odds, the giant Goliath could be defeated, then the theory of survival of the fittest is ruled out. That particular story alone is enough evidence that—as young, inexperienced, and small-in-physique David was in comparison to Goliath—confidence and survival come from how one perceives the size and strength of their God. In other words, David never considered Goliath's massive size or strength; He put His confidence in God's power to bring down his enemy.

Even some well-known biologists and scientists have proven through their comparisons between evolution and faith that *nothing* or *no one* is bigger than the Founder! That's really what you need—confidence in God and who He says you are and what you can do through His power! The Bible declares, "For I can do all things through Christ who gives me strength!" (Philippians 4:13 NLT). So, the next time a problem arises that looks too great to overcome, I suggest you make this declaration: "Father, I will not consider the problem; I will consider your Word." The victory lies in believing in what the Word says about your situation. Remember, Jesus defeated Satan with the Word!

One definition of *confidence* states that it is a relation of trust or intimacy. In relation to God, this means that you must make a conscious effort to fellowship with Him daily to be able to trust and confide in Him. Another definition states that *confidence* is faith or belief that one will act in a right, proper, or effective way. Again, in relation to God, this means that for you to have confidence in Him, you must have faith that He knows what He has called you to be, achieve, and victoriously overcome in life. This requires that you believe that He will direct you on the *best* path for your life.

With that said, to do anything meaningful in life, you must have confidence (trust) in something or someone and be motivated to pursue your goals. If you believe you can do something, your confidence (in your goals) will motivate you to try, and you will most likely succeed, even if you have to try multiple times. Each time you fail, you learn what doesn't work, which is considered progress itself. Then upon examining the problem, you can make adjustments that will either get you closer to finding a resolution or actual success the next time. On the other hand, if you believe that you cannot do something, your lack of confidence will inevitably create failure. What you perceive to happen for you will produce either success or failure.

In psychology, predicting someone else's fate or directly predicting your own fate is known as the self-fulling prophecy. Refuse to surrender to failure. Remember this: it is better to try and fail at something than to succeed doing absolutely nothing. *Effort* is the force that propels your vision into reality. In times past, we have learned of many visionaries who didn't have two nickels to rub together; nevertheless, they became successful simply because they tried.

> **It is better to try and fail at something than to succeed doing absolutely nothing.**
>
> **Effort is the force that propels your vision into reality.**

The Handbook states in Proverbs 23:7 (KJV), "As a man thinketh in his heart, so is he." You might desire to be a teacher, nurse, pianist, or gourmet chef, but if you don't believe that it is possible, then you will never seriously apply yourself to learn how to be exceptional at it. Moreover, your desire may be to live a righteous and holy lifestyle, but without ultimately putting your confidence in God to help you accomplish godly living, it just won't happen for you. Before you can accomplish anything, you must first *believe* that you can do it, then you must put in the *work*. Belief and hard work, not merely possessing money, will take you to your desired destination.

The true confidence that lasts a lifetime—whether in your professional career, family life, personal friendships, or some other area—comes from developing a *trusting* relationship with the Founder. To gain confidence as an employee, you must be willing to put all your faith and trust in Him. Confidence is something that you must strive to attain for yourself; nobody can give it to you, no matter how much they try to build you up. And you will not become confident overnight.

It is developed gradually over time with lots of training, meditating, studying, and practicing scriptural affirmations in the Handbook. It is only when you put effort in studying the Handbook can you learn the mind and will of the Founder.

Many inspired employees of the company can attest that you will become the books that you read, the movies that you watch, and the people with whom you associate. This process of becoming does take some time. Nevertheless, if you will commit to studying the Handbook consistently and associate yourself with employees who are dedicated to the Founder and His company's mission, you will soon be able to confidently make decisions with the mind of the Founder.

When you begin the process of confidence-building, you will start like an infant on milk. And like all babies, as you grow spiritually, you will soon begin eating solid foods and will no longer need the nutrition designed for infants. Your spiritual growth will be evident as you become fully knowledgeable of the Founder's will for your life. You will then become confident in making sound decisions that are in the best interest of yourself, your family, and the company. This process is called *spiritual maturity*, and it has nothing to do with your chronological age. No one gets to this point quickly or automatically because of physical aging. Building confidence is a journey. And like all journeys, it takes time, patience, and proper nourishment to reach and maintain your appointed destination.

---

**Building confidence is a journey. And like all journeys, it takes time, patience, and proper nourishment to reach and maintain your appointed destination.**

---

An example of the importance of development and its correlation to time would be the planting and growth of a mustard seed. This tiny seed, which is one to two millimeters in size, produces a large ten-to-fifteen-foot bush. A mustard bush takes approximately eight weeks to reach half of its full height from a seed. There is no way to rush the growth of this plant. It must have its ordained amount of time and nourishment to reach full maturity.

The same development process applies with each new employee who is highered in the company. One of the amazing things about true confidence is that it breeds confidence in others. Confident employees don't have to push their will on others. When an employee has true confidence, it gives him or her energy, empowerment, and strength. This type of confidence is known as God-confidence!

When employees have God-confidence, they don't seek their own will, but God's. As they use their gifts and talents to bring glory to God—when the pressures of life try to come in—they don't buckle under pressure because they *know* who they are and why they are doing what they do: to bring glory to God. When your confidence is in God, you will be better able to perform your job and execute the company's mission, which is to win others to the company. Your confidence will not be in yourself, and you will boldly say, "In God we boast all the day long, and praise thy name forever. Se'lah." (Psalm 44:8 KJV).

> **When employees have God-confidence, they
> don't seek their own will, but God's.**

When you put your confidence in God, you will start moving toward your God-given goals to accomplish whatever He has called you to do and be, whether it is to be a spouse, parent, mentor, missionary, Christian artist, or the like.

## Moral Corruptness Exuding Itself as Confident

In 1 Kings chapter 16, you will find an example of a person who was morally corrupt but presented herself as self-confident. Jezebel—beautiful, charming, sensual, sexy, and fashionable—was the wife of King Ahab, ruler of Israel. But with all her creative attributes, she was also overly self-confident, controlling, manipulative, deceitful, greedy, and excessive. Jezebel was wicked, to say the least! When it came to power, she used all her physical, social, and economic assets to get *whatever* she wanted. Everything she did had to be over-the-top for self-gratification.

As a mark of rebellion against God and spiritual authority, Jezebel seduced and killed all the prophets of old, except Elijah, and all but one of her grandchildren, to manipulate and control situations and leaders to do evil. In fact, not even her husband, Ahab, who was the ruler of Israel, would stand up and stop her from committing criminal and scandalous acts. The only reason she could not kill Elijah and her youngest baby grandson is that God protected them from her.

By instinct, a man possesses a need to protect and provide for his household. He has a need to be respected by the members of his household, especially his wife. Rightfully so, one would think that Ahab would have exercised his godly authority over his wife since, as a man, he was ordained by God to lead his household as a husband and father. But Ahab was a coward who did not hold Jezebel accountable for her actions; nor did he take his position seriously as the ruler over Israel. Instead, he gave up his mind, will, and power as a husband and king to follow his wife, allowing her to teach false doctrine and sexually seduce the church of Thyatira and kill anyone who got in her way (read Revelation 2:20–23).

It is worth noting that Jezebel's sexual influence allured approximately ten million male Israelites from serving God the Founder into a lifestyle of worshipping the gods of Baal and Ashtaroth. This explains how sex can be used as a powerful tool to turn a man (or woman) and an entire nation away from God's purpose for their lives.

The Handbook teaches us in Proverbs 26:4 (ESV), "Answer not a fool according to his folly, lest you be like him yourself." Ahab did not have to answer to Jezebel; he needed to rightfully *take* his position of leadership as the head of his household and as the ruler of Israel and lead with love and righteousness. If he had done that, Jezebel would have been unable to mislead the people or kill the prophets and her grandchildren. In the final analysis, God's wrath came upon Ahab first, as the head, then Jezebel; the dogs ate her flesh by the wall of Jezreel (read 1 Kings 16:23). The moral of the story is this: self-confident people who are obsessed with power will eventually become weak and lose it. Additionally, those who are complicit, like Ahab, will receive God's judgement. God is looking for men and women who will boldly confront evil people, not bow down to them.

> **Self-confident people who are obsessed with power
> will eventually become weak and lose it.**

The spirit of Jezebel is one of the reasons why abortion, divorce, homosexuality, racial profiling, violent rioting, government and business corruption, false teachings, and all other types of injustices (or hatred and rebellion) are prevalent today in our society. People don't want to be told what to do, even if it comes from the right source (the Bible) to protect their best interest in the long run. Some pro-choice individuals or groups shout, "It's my choice what I do!"—never taking into consideration that a helpless, innocent unborn life who needs protection is inside them or inside the womb of their girlfriend, daughter, wife, sister, or friend. Neither do they stop to consider how it will ultimately affect the father of the child nor the mother's mental, physical, or overall life in the long run. (We need to seriously think about the issues that upper management has enforced with the help of Planned Parenthood—selling the idea of abortion as a method of contraceptive to girls and women while increasing their revenue. We need to also consider how upper management is striving to redefine marriage by allowing people who chose alternate lifestyles to legally marry and acquire the same rights as husbands and wives, which goes against the principles of God, the Creator of life. Moreover, the 2021 insurrection of the United States Capitol building was a horrific crime against the 117th United States Congress that should have been just cause for the impeachment and imprisonment of upper management. No leader can make America great by creating chaos and division among the citizens. The only way a leader can ever make this country great is by persuading citizens to *love one another* and *work together.*) In Romans 13:8 (NKJV), the Apostle Paul makes this recommendation:

> Owe no one anything except to love one another, for he who loves another has fulfilled the law.

Remember, love is the only solution to cure hatred and rebellion.

The spirit of Jezebel is one of the reasons why many people in the church are still in bondage and under burdensome yokes by false prophets who speak wealth and riches over the people—so-called prophesying (lies) to God's people while milking them dry (all in the name of Jesus) of their financial resources and stripping them of their emotional, physical, and spiritual confidence and strength in the Founder. These false prophets toy with popular cliches, such as

- "You'll never go where you don't sow!"
- "Plant a seed to meet your need!"
- "If you want a blessing, you've got to give—until it hurts!"

They use these loud and ridiculous cliches aggressively to pressure good-hearted Christians to empty their purses and wallets just so they can become rich, powerful, and famous. These false prophets are ruthless, greedy dogs who never get enough!

> Yea, they are greedy dogs which can *never* have enough, and they are shepherds without wisdom: they have all gone after their pleasure, each one to his unjust gain, they are all the same. (Isaiah 56:11 KJV; emphasis added)

If they could suck blood out of a turnip, they would try!

This is the type of oppression that inflicts more hurt on those (employees of the Founder) who come to church already hurting—tearing down their family finances, peace of mind, happy marriages and homes, confidence, faith in God and in themselves—preventing them from pursuing and attaining much-needed personal and professional goals. Listen! Putting all your income into the church (the physical building, that is) is not going to meet all your needs. You have to use common sense to save some of your hard-earned money to take care of and invest in yourself, your children, and your elderly parents too. This is the wise and enjoyable thing to do! Besides, nobody wants to go to work just to give it *all* away. A person who is in their right mind would never agree to do that! In the book of Proverbs 12:11 (KJV), it states, "He that tilleth his land shall be satisfied with bread [to eat]: but he that followeth vain persons is void of understanding" (emphasis added).

Sadly, most people who are easily influenced (or brainwashed) by false prophets pay everybody but themselves! The truth is that the false prophet is not going to be around when you find yourself broke, busted, and disgusted because you gave into his or her flattering punch lines regarding giving. Be sensible and keep enjoying your life! Don't give in to the high pressure of so-called spiritual leaders *selling* the Word of God for their own material gain. The truth is this: God is not for sale; nor is the house of God to be used as a marketplace! Jesus emphasized this in Matthew 21:13 (NKJV), when he said, "My house shall be called a house of prayer, but you have made it a den of thieves." The house of God is supposed to be a place of continuous healing, worship, fellowship, and learning, not a place to take advantage of people.

---

**God is not for sale; nor is the house of God to be used as a marketplace!**

---

In the first part of 2 Corinthians 9:7, the Bible emphatically instructs us *not* to give reluctantly (with a grudge) or in response to pressure to meet an urgent need (for ourselves, loved ones, or the spiritual leader). What God is saying here is that the act of giving should be a "voluntary" sacrifice that is from *your* heart; it is not offered because of an urgent need that you have or pressure from the pulpit leaders. High-pressure tactics and instant gratification should not be known in the house of God or among God's employees.

The second part of this same scripture (2 Corinthians 9:7 AMP) says that "God loves a cheerful giver and delights in the one whose heart is in his gift!" God wants you to give according to what *you* have already purposed in your heart to give because that will keep *you* cheerful, and God loves a cheerful giver. Employees of the Founder cannot be cheerful if the leaders are using force—through smooth talk, charm, and aggressive speech—to pressure them to give monetarily more than they are ready, willing, or able to give until it hurts, or until they are in desperate need. Even if a person is able to give, he or she should not be pressured to do so. The Holy Spirit will lead a person to give generously.

Giving *all* that you have is not a wise thing to do because it causes you to remain in the impoverished condition that you are presently in, making it impossible for you to properly budget your current monthly expenses and save or invest for the future. It also causes you to feel guilty, ashamed, and abused (spiritually and financially) when you are forced to give more than you have already purposed in your heart to give. This applies to the rich and poor alike. So, you don't have to give outside your comfort zone or financial ability to move the heart of your Father. God will bless you simply because you are a "cheerful giver" of what you have already purposed in your heart to give and because He said that "He watches over those He loves." And yes, God loves you—unconditionally!

The spirit of Jezebel also has caused so many marriages in Hollywood (and around the world) to be on the rocks and have even destroyed many of them. This wicked spirit has caused many of our youth to follow satanic influence through the internet, text messaging, music, magazines, television, games, and other forms of communication and entertainment. In Mark 7:15 (KJV), Jesus said this to the crowd: "Nothing from without a man, that entering into him can defile him: but the things which come out of him, those are they that defile the man." That being said, once the spirit of Jezebel is demonstrated through a person, he or she becomes defiled in their behavior.

According to *The Free Dictionary*, the term *arrogant* means "having or displaying a sense of overbearing self-worth or self-importance." When people take on an arrogant spirit, they start living a life outside of the Founder's will. This means that people who are outside of the Founder's will automatically live under Satan's influence like Jezebel did. An arrogant spirit is very self-centered, and its focus and energy are driven by self-gratification that says, "I want it *now!*" This spirit never takes the Founder's ways into consideration. It is selfish, angry, and unforgiving; it never gives off an ounce of positive energy but rather steals your joy and peace of mind.

When the spirit of arrogance overtakes an environment, it fills the atmosphere with a thick negative cloud that prevents well-meaning people from flourishing in all that the Founder purposed for their lives. Proverbs 18:6 (NIV) states, "The lips of fools bring them strife, and their mouths invite a beating." That says it all right there!

Remember that God-confidence attracts and leads to a successful path, but arrogance repels and causes people to be ensnared in darkness. As an employee of the Founder, you don't want to ever find yourself repelling anyone, thereby blocking their chances of becoming highered in the company and becoming all that they can be for God's glory.

> **God-confidence attracts and leads to a successful path, but arrogance repels and causes people to be ensnared in darkness.**

## How Does God See You?

How you see yourself has a direct correlation to your level of confidence and long-term success in life. People who perform well in their vocation usually have a higher level of confidence than those with low levels. For the short term, this holds true regardless of whether a person is a child of God. But in the long term, if a person is not established in God, they will end up losing sight of the big picture, and their life will begin a downward spiral, publicly and privately. How you see yourself stems from your thoughts and feelings about yourself and the environment out of which you've come.

One important reason so many people have problems feeling good about themselves and struggle to accomplish their life goals is they allow the negative words of those who speak over them to consume their mind, which causes them to lose confidence in God and in themselves. You've heard the old adage, "Sticks and stones may break my bones, but your words will never hurt me!" That's so untrue. Perhaps your mom, dad, a former teacher, coach, friend, or enemy said some hurtful things to you that got stuck in your mind, and you just can't seem to shake it. You've tried positive-thinking techniques, but you still find yourself empty inside. That's because positive thinking alone cannot sustain a hungry soul; it has no *spiritual* force behind it. Only faith-filled words from the Handbook can fill the void that you feel inside and give birth to a new way of life for you. In John 6:63 (NASB), it is written (emphasis added),

> It is the Spirit who gives life; the flesh profits nothing; the words that I have spoken to you are Spirit and life.

Instead of seeing yourself through the eyes of others (the way the world sees you), the Founder wants you to forgive and forget about what they said about you and focus on how He sees you. The words that God has spoken about you produce abundant life in you. Below is a list of scriptures that you can read aloud to boost your confidence in God and know who you are in Him.

- I am a new creature in Christ (2 Corinthians 5:17).
- I am a joint heir with Christ (Romans 8:17).
- I am the righteousness of God in Jesus Christ (2 Corinthians 5:21).
- I am forgiven of all my sins and washed in the Blood (Ephesians 1:7).
- I am a doer of the Word and blessed in my actions (James 1:22).
- I am fearfully and wonderfully made, and my soul knows that full well (Psalm 139:14).
- I am complete in Christ who is the Head of all principality and power (Colossians 2:10).
- I am far from oppression, and fear does not come near me (Isaiah 54:14).
- I am born of God, and the evil one does not touch me (1 John 5:18).
- I am redeemed from the curse of sin, sickness, and poverty (Deuteronomy 28:15–68).
- I am healed by the stripes of Jesus (Isaiah 53:5).
- I am loved by God (1 John 4:19).

Stand confidently behind the vision of who God has called you to be. See yourself as God sees you! He fashioned you as a special and unique person with talents and gifts that are to be used to bring His name glory! He loves you despite your past or what someone else has said about you! Take a good look in the mirror at the confident person the Founder created in the image of Himself. And thank Him for the confidence boost!

## Benefits of Living with Confidence in God

Like working on a regular job for an earthly boss, there are benefits to living in confidence with God. As an employee of the Founder, God has a benefits package for you that comes from your connection with Him as His son or daughter. Below is a list of the benefits of living with confidence in God:

- He gives you joy and strength (Proverbs 31:25; Nehemiah 8:9).
- He gives you power to overcome and succeed in any situation (Zechariah 4:6; 1 John 4:4).
- He gives you peace in the midst of any trial (Psalm 119:165; Isaiah 32:17; Isaiah 26:3).
- He gives you long life and prosperity (Proverbs 3:2; Psalm 91:6; Psalm 84:11).
- He comforts you (Psalm 71:21).
- He gives you the desires of your heart (Psalm 37:3–5).
- He helps and protects you from all harm (Psalm 121:1–4).

When you understand the desires of the Founder and how His desires benefit you personally, you will not waste any time seeking gainful employment in His company. And in doing so, you will be well on your way to walking and living your life in complete confidence in God.

## An Example of the God Kind of Confidence

There is a true story in the Bible that demonstrates this level of true confidence and how chronological age, cultural background, and race have no bearing on it. This story is about how Satan made one of his new employees a ruler over many lands and how, in due course, God turned the ruler's heart toward His employees.

In Daniel chapter 3, there were three teenage Hebrew princes whose names originally were Hananiah (Yah is gracious), Mishael (Who is like Yah), and Azariah (Yah has helped)—all having a godly meaning behind their names. These young men were among the most brilliant and highly favored employees of the Founder, and they were sold out to worshipping *only* Him. But once they were selected to be trained for three years to serve King Nebuchadnezzar, the chief officer gave them Babylonian names—Shadrach, Meshach, and Abednego—hoping that they would forget their identity as children of the Founder to accept Babylonian practices. (Satan has always used change as a means to get people to turn away from God and His original purpose for their lives.)

One day, King Nebuchadnezzar built a golden idol that stood ninety-feet high and nine-feet wide and called all the princes, governors, captains, and rulers of the land to come and see his crafty work. When all the people saw the golden statue that King Nebuchadnezzar had carved, he ordered them to bow down and worship it. This did not sit well with the Hebrew princes, so they refused to bow down to the golden idol. They confidently told the ruler that they would not bow down and worship any idols because the Founder did not approve of such things. This statement made King Nebuchadnezzar so angry that he threatened to throw them into the fiery furnace should they disobey his command. But these Hebrew princes were uncompromisingly courageous. They stood their ground and told the king that their Boss (God) would save them if He wanted them to escape death. They further told the king that if their Boss decided not to rescue them from the fire, they would remain obedient to Him and would not bow down to anyone or anything other than Him.

The king became furious at the young men's position and ordered his soldiers to put them into the furnace. He even had the heat increased seven times hotter than normal. The heat from the fiery furnace was so hot that the soldiers who threw the Hebrew princes into the furnace were killed instantly by the intense heat. As the furnace blazed, the Hebrew princes were seen standing, holding hands, and praying in the middle of the fire without even a strand of their hair singed. Their clothes were intact, and they came out "smelling like roses"!

The king gazed into the furnace with disbelief and amazement as he observed that the Founder's protection had kept the young princes from getting burned up in the fire. This arrogant king did not believe what he had seen, so he asked someone standing close to him in bewilderment, "Did we not throw three men into the fire?"

"Yes," replied the bystander.

The king then replied in shock, "How is it that four men are standing in the fire?" (The fourth man whom the king saw in the fire was Jesus, the Son of Man.)

Everyone was astounded at this miracle they had just witnessed. The king's fear of the Boss prompted him to command everyone to serve God only, and he appointed Shadrach, Meshach, and Abednego over the entire province! He then warned everyone in the province to keep silent about what they had just witnessed; otherwise, he would chop them to pieces, anyone who spoke against these young princes. What a way to show reverence for the Founder!

The attitude and actions of these young men are the perfect demonstration of true confidence in the Founder, which every employee of the company should exemplify. As an employee of the Founder, your confidence should be so strong in Him that no circumstance could ever overwhelm you. Like the three Hebrew princes, you must stand courageously under trials and say,

> If we are thrown into the blazing furnace, the God (Yahweh) we serve is able to rescue us from it, and He will rescue us from your hand, O king. But even if He does not, we want you to know, O king, that we will *not* serve your gods or worship the image of gold you have set up. (Daniel 3:17–18 NIV; emphasis added)

No matter what trials come your way, keep your confidence in the Founder! Don't let Satan misplace your identity! Always know who you belong to and see yourself as God sees you! Praise Him as if you've already got the victory, because He *will* be with you until the very end! The Founder will never fail His faith-filled employees!

*Cast not away therefore your confidence, which hath great recompense of reward. For ye have need of patience, that, after ye have done the will of God, ye might receive the promise. For yet a little while, and He that shall come will come, and will not tarry.*

—Hebrews 10:35–37 (KJV)

# Chapter 12

## Motivation on the Job

Sometimes life has a way of knocking you down, but it's up to you to decide whether you're going to get up or stay down. The fact of the matter is this: everybody falls into a slump once in a while and needs someone to help pull them out of it. One of the best things about working for the Founder is that He always has someone in the company to come alongside you to pick you up, dust you off, and give you a helping hand. This dispels the myth that you're alone in God's assignment, for you're never alone.

As employees of the Founder, you and I are specially made to encourage each other daily, especially when one of us feels lonely, hopeless, inadequate, and in need of spiritual uplifting. When another employee experiences challenges that can negatively affect their daily Christian walk, this is a wonderful opportunity to reach out to them and remind them that not only does the Founder care about him or her, but you care too. Theodore Roosevelt once said, "People don't care how much you know until they know how much you care." The biggest blessing in our lives is simply the presence of people who care for us, love us, and see us beyond ourselves. This leads to the next three subtopics of discussion: how to stay motivated in your assignment, the hindrances to staying motivated, and how to get out of a rut.

> **The biggest blessing in our lives is simply the presence of people who care for us, love us, and see us beyond ourselves.**

## How to Stay Motivated in Your Assignment

Remember when I stated earlier that without love, nothing can survive? Well, the same is true when it comes to staying motivated on both your secular and spiritual job assignment. The *first* and best way to stay motivated and encourage your fellow employees in the Founder's company is to show genuine love and concern for them and toward yourself. It has been said that love is an action word; if it does nothing, then it isn't love. By appropriately demonstrating your love toward others and yourself, you build them up and cause them to change in ways they never thought could happen; in turn, you build yourself up as the motivator. Pleasant words are wonderful, but when you walk in love, your sacrificial commitment holds much more weight than mere words.

> **Pleasant words are wonderful, but when you walk in love, your sacrificial commitment holds much more weight than mere words.**

For example, when the religious leaders took the woman (whom they caught in the very act of adultery) to Jesus, they tried to convince Him of all the reasons that she should be stoned. Instead of having her stoned, Jesus lovingly protected her and offered her the gift of salvation. The message surrounding earthly employment and its comparison to the Founder's employees is similar in this example. The intent of the above example is clear. When Jesus showed the woman love and acceptance, she became motivated to give up her disgraceful lifestyle to become a committed employee of the Founder! However difficult it may have become, the woman's positive response to Jesus's acceptance of her caused Him to remain motivated to continue on His assignment too! You see, everybody wants to feel loved, accepted, and appreciated, which is a reward every employee desires to obtain in their job assignment.

The *second* thing you can do to motivate others is to provide an active listening ear that allows fellow employees of the company to share their problems, struggles, and ideas in confidence. Listening to the concerns of others causes understanding and wisdom to come, which enables you, the listener, to provide effective solutions to their problems and generate witty ideas to help them succeed in their assignment, as well as your own.

Just as we go to God in prayer (He listens to the heart of the matter and answers our prayers), we should live out this example in our efforts to encourage others. David declared in Psalm 34:1 (KJV), "I sought the Lord, and he answered me, and delivered me from all my fears." Listening helps you learn valuable information about others and their circumstances, builds meaningful relationships, helps you get along with others, helps you understand them and their needs, helps you come up with specific solutions to overcome problems and provide successful solutions, and helps develop you as an employee on the job for the Founder, as well as your secular vocation. All in all, listening motivates progress!

The *third* thing you can do to stay motivated is to eagerly pursue the company's mission. This requires knowing your particular calling or assignment and working enthusiastically where you are right now. The late Walter Percy Chrysler, a self-trained engineer who assisted in forming Chrysler, once said, "The real secret of success is enthusiasm." The word *enthusiastic* refers to your passion in life. It also means, "God within"—if you are an employee (believer) of the Founder. Thus, if you are a believer of Yahshua (Christ), then Yahweh (God) is within you. This means that your passion and pursuit is God!

It has been found that employees who are enthusiastic about their assignment are energetic and upbeat, enjoy their workday, and perform quality work. Also, these employees remain flexible enough to help others in their assignment as needed. When you are diligently working on your assignment, you remain in a useful state of mind at all times.

The *fourth* and final way to stay motivated in your assignment is to walk in a positive spirit. The late Mary Kay Ash, founder of Mary Kay Inc., used the golden rule according to Matthew 7:12 (NLT), "Do to others whatever you would like them to do to you," as the foundation for her company, and she became quite successful. Your positive attitude has a trickle-down effect on others, and it definitely works! Smiling, complimenting others, and asking if you could lend a helping hand while working around other employees of the Founder sets an atmosphere of peace, joy, happiness, and contentment on the job. These positive expressions will automatically remind them who is behind your ray of sunshine!

## Ten Hindrances to Staying Motivated

1.  Boredom
2.  Loneliness and isolation from society
3.  Lack of concentration and interest
4.  A self-defeated attitude or negative attitude toward others
5.  Impatience and hopelessness
6.  Slow financial and material donations
7.  Being burdened with work
8.  Complaining and unfocused company
9.  Plentiful work and few laborers
10. Struggles with the flesh

### How to Get Out of a Rut

Remember, problems and personal failures are temporary. All things must come to an end. This too shall pass. As long as you are working toward progress, your life will change for the better. Nothing meant for your growth ever remains the same. Good people will eventually show up and assist you when they see your honesty and commitment to your vision and how it will benefit others. So, don't ever make a permanent decision (to give up) when facing a temporary setback. Remember, your setback could be a set *up* for a greater comeback! Satan's plots cannot override God's master plans for your life! If God can take Joseph from the pit of Egyptian imprisonment to the palace to govern over the people, then he can set you up too! Just don't quit! "There is a time for everything, and a season for every activity under the heavens" (Ecclesiastes 3:1 NIV).

Be patient but persistent in prayer and preparation during the in-between moments of life. Keep praying, planning, learning, growing, and preparing while facing challenges and opportunities that are before you until God gives you exactly what you long for. Henry Hartman once said, "Success is nothing more than preparation meeting opportunity." Therefore, continue to keep your hands to the plow because "in due season you shall reap if you faint not" (Galatians 6:9 KJV).

Remind yourself why you came to Christ in the first place. Keep your eye on the prize—aim for the higher calling or purpose of God for your life (read Philippians 3:14). Write a vision statement on a blackboard near your workspace. This helps keep you focused on working in your calling and mission for doing what you do. Do not allow material gain to be your main focus. When you take good care of people (clients, church members, and staff), God will, in turn, take care of you. Every morning try getting up a few minutes early to start your day with prayer and meditate on what your goal is for that day. Reaffirm daily what you are pressing toward and go for it! Remember that diligent hands rule! "The thoughts of the diligent tend only to plenty; but the thoughts of everyone who is hasty only to poverty" (Proverbs 21:5 NIV).

Keep a track record of successes from your church members (if you are a pastor or leader), business clients, or friend testimonials and emails that you've had already. Ask for periodic evaluations from church members, friends, and people who have worked with you. "Know the state of your flocks, and put your heart into caring for your herds" (Proverbs 27:23 NLT). Find out what you've been doing right and wrong, and then ask for advice. Keep believing in God to help you make practical plans and invent new ways of doing things. Then execute your plans. "Give instruction to a wise man, and he will be still wiser; teach a just man, and he will increase in learning" (Proverbs 9:9 NKJV).

If you are struggling with discipline, confidence, financial planning/budgeting, problem-solving, or some other personal issue, *get help* immediately. Seek wisdom from a few employees of the Founder who can keep you accountable for your assignment and instruct you. You need a few mentors who are gifted in various subject areas to help you stay on track with and improve on your ministry endeavors. This will help you set priorities and become more organized. Don't run from your problems or wait until they become worse to seek help. Do something about it as soon as you see it coming. Proverbs 27:12 (TLB) states, "A sensible man watches for problems ahead and prepares to meet them. The simpleton never looks and suffers the consequences."

Always maintain an attitude of hope for brighter days ahead. Know that with God's guidance, you will overcome and thrive! Repeat Romans 8:37 (KJV) aloud daily: "Nay, in all these things we are more than conquerors through him that loved us!" Remember, whatever, whoever, or wherever you place your faith is where you will go. Faith brings you to your destination. Thus, walk in confidence toward the path that leads to life, blessings, and success in the Founder.

> **Nothing meant for your growth ever remains the same.**

In conclusion, motivation is a powerful tool for any company, and since the Founder created it, He expects to see all His employees give and receive encouragement from one another. Regardless of your spiritual vocation as an employee of the Founder, your primary focus should not be on earning a large paycheck and bonuses like earthly employees do. Instead, your focus should be on the things that keep the mission of the company moving forward, first and foremost. Love and concern for those whom you minister should be the motivating force that compels you forward in successfully accomplishing your God-given assignment on a daily basis.

> **Whatever, whoever, or wherever you place
> your faith is where you will go.**
>
> ---
>
> **Faith brings you into your destination.**

*Keep on loving each other as brothers.*

—Hebrews 13:1 (NIV)

# Chapter 13

## Teamwork—Together Everyone Achieves More

You've heard the slogan, "Teamwork makes the dream work." Well, this is true in every relationship where there are two or more persons involved. Since the Founder initiated and endorsed families first, it is relevant to conclude that teamwork begins at home. In the Handbook, Genesis 2:18 (NKJV) informs us of the Founder's decision to create the first family: "And the Lord God said, 'It is not good that man should be alone; I will make him a helper comparable to him.'" Thus, we know that in this passage of scripture, the man was Adam, and his helper was Eve. The Founder made the man (husband) the leader and the woman (wife) his helper. The definition of the word *helper* is "a person who contributes to the fulfillment of a need or the furtherance of an effort or purpose." Another meaning of the word *helper* is "one who helps, aids, assists, or relieves another."

With this said, in order to have an effective team, there must first be a leader—such as the husband leading the wife and children, the coach leading the team, the president leading the country or company, and the pastor leading the flock—and second, some helpers or assistants, such as wives, children, athletes, and employees. These fundamental roles are needed to make up or complete the team or family. Successful teams have fundamental qualities: clear purpose, clear roles and responsibilities, good practices (open communication, decision making, and problem solving, etc.), and good relationships (within and outside the work environment).

In today's society, research shows that many women lead their families because the husband or the father of their children is passively involved, absent, deceased, or unemployed. It is important to say that some men are passively involved, absent, or unemployed by force due to an illness, disability, lack of education, or uncontrollable circumstance, not necessarily by choice. Also, out-of-wedlock childbirths and divorces (either by force or personal choice against God's Handbook) are major issues that have caused many women to suffer the consequences of having to take full responsibility of the home—which has caused poverty (instability) financially, physically, emotionally, intellectually, and behaviorally among children (US Department of Health and Human Services 1990). Regarding women leading the family, you can see why this is not the Founder's original or best plan for the family because both women and children will have unmet needs. Women need a husband for companionship, emotional and financial support, protection, and sexual intimacy. Children need their fathers' love, protection, financial provision, and guidance. Both women and children feel safe when the leader husband/father is in the home, exercising his godly role. Nonetheless, due to sin, many families have to learn cooperative ways of blending together in order to work toward accomplishing shared goals.

**Top Reasons Why People Are Ineffective on Teams**

1. Poor leadership skills
2. Unresolved conflicts from the past hinder current relationships
3. Poor communication skills due to negative emotions
4. Being a poor example
5. Too many chiefs, not enough Indians

6. Jealousy or competitiveness
7. Outside influences
8. The Lone Ranger syndrome

This above list of negative behaviors is very damaging and destructive to any partnership, whether in a marriage and family, sports, church, business, or friendship. The Founder grieves when we, His children, model after these insensitive, egotistical, uncaring, and stubborn patterns of behavior. For example, after graduating from North Carolina Agricultural and Technical State University, my wife accepted a position as the executive secretary at a North Carolina based Fortune 500 company. Prior to showing up for work daily, Victoria would pray, meditate on a Bible scripture, and listen to praise music so that she could professionally perform her secretarial duties and report to her immediate boss, who was the operations manager. Victoria described her boss's personality as cold, callous, unfriendly, and withdrawn. My wife tried to utilize several techniques that she had learned from her experience as a Christian and psychology graduate to influence effective communication and a good working relationship with her boss. But his attitude remained the same. (You see, it's a choice.) So, after being on the job for a month, during an afternoon lunch break, she decided to walk off, and never return. An hour after Victoria quit, she received a call from the human resource director at the corporate office telling her that the corporate office team had already figured out why she quit because they had lost several secretaries within the same year. Moreover, the hiring team requested Victoria's return, and offered to double her hourly pay rate, but she told them that she'd rather work for less money, and for a boss who has a positive attitude, shows an interest in (and enjoys) communicating and working with his employees (team), copes well under pressure, and takes responsibility for his actions, attitude, and team.

My wife accepted their apology, but she decided to uphold godly principles. Proverbs 22:24 (NKJV) says, "Make no friendship with an angry man, and with a furious man do not go." That day, Victoria's decision showed the corporate team how a leader's negative attitude can decrease employee retention rates. Additionally, her actions helped the human resource team realize how important it is for them to select a qualified manager who possesses godly characteristics, such as good people skills to effectively work well with his or her team, so that the company's goals can be accomplished; and not select a person based on their technical skills alone.

The Bible says that these harmful behaviors must not even be named among us, His employees (read 1 Corinthians 15:33). Next, I will list some guidelines that can help you deal with situations that are causing trouble in your personal or professional relationships.

**Effective Ways to Resolve Conflict**

In Matthew 18:15 (NKJV), Jesus instructs us how to conduct ourselves should an offense arise among us (emphasis added):

> If your brother [or sister] sins against you, go and tell him his fault between you and him *alone*; if he hears you, you have gained your brother. But, if he will not hear, take with you one or two more, that by the mouth of two or three witnesses every word may be established. And if he refuses to hear them, tell it to the church. But if he refuses even to hear the church, let him be to you like a heathen and a tax collector.

Here are some healthy guidelines for good communication to effectively resolve conflicts in any relationship.

1. Go directly to the person in private to address the problem, no third parties (yet).
2. Separate the problem from the person. Avoid making personal attacks that can embarrass or ridicule the other person.
3. Consider the other person's concerns, interests, and needs as well as your own. Be respectful, sensitive, and unselfish.
4. Allow each other to speak without interruptions. Come to a mutual agreement on each issue stated. Avoid bringing up the past.
5. Negotiate for mutual satisfaction. The outcome should be a win-win solution for both parties.

6. If you fail to resolve the issue the first time you try, be patient and let the issue rest. Pray for understanding and peace; then try again with the help of a trained or gifted biblical counselor.

7. If biblical counseling does not work, simply cut ties with the person. Realize that some people are not spiritually mature enough to handle problems as a result of their personal choice to remain emotionally handicapped. For some, staying angry and unforgiving makes them feel as though they have power over those with whom they have a conflict, but they are delusional; and only fooling themselves.

In other words, if the person with whom you have a conflict listens to you, the issue will be lovingly resolved, and work can resume as usual. However, if the person with whom you have a conflict refuses to listen to you and to the counselors who are mediating to resolve the issue, simply let him or her go. You don't have to remain in bondage to a person's anger. Kindly give him or her walking papers.

It's better to retain cohesiveness with the rest of the team members than to keep a hotheaded know-it-all on your team. This is the case in any relationship. One bad apple can ruin the whole team and its goals.

I recall a time when my daughter Sara was a member of the volleyball team at her former school. Their team was indeed the most talented out of all the teams in the league. But, when their team made it to the Varsity Volleyball Finals, they came in last place. The team that was expected to place last in the Finals ended up placing third. I firmly believe that the reason the outcome was victorious for the team that had the worst record in the league was due to effective teamwork. The girls maintained a good attitude, listened to their coach's instructions, trusted each other, and were able to make the necessary adjustments to defeat seven teams. No matter how bad their team performed, the coach kept encouraging her players, and the players gained the faith they needed to hold on to secure the bronze medal. Contrarily, when Sara's team began to fall behind the other teams, their team captain would lose her composure and start arguing with her teammates, and the team would fall apart on the court.

Arguments break down the spirit and strength of a team. Without support and positive behavioral norms, a team cannot be successful. Sometimes the best leader on a team is not the person with the most talent, but the one who has the ability to remain calm and encouraging.

> Therefore encourage one another and build each other up, just as in fact you are doing. (I Thessalonians 5:11 KJV)

**Seven Principles for Effective Teamwork**

With teamwork, there are seven major principles that all employees of the Founder should exercise at all times when they are working with fellow employees. They are essential for various areas of employment such as work, worship, leisure, and family life. These seven skills are as follows:

1.  Respect. Trust the leader to lead, and teammates should follow.
2.  Listen. Gain a good understanding of the matter.
3.  Share. Give and take advice as necessary.
4.  Help. Find solutions to one another's problems.
5.  Question. Gain an understanding and execute.
6.  Participate. Hold down your position well.
7.  Encourage. This increases belief and faith in one another.

Putting these seven principles into practice will promote respect, trust, confidence, cooperation, communication, and compromise among teammates to accomplish the team's goals. This concept is also true with the Founder's team of employees, whether in marriage and family, church, business, sports, or outreach ministries. The Founder designed each employee's work to be a part of the whole. In this same manner, He designed the human body.

**The Body Is a Team of Many Members**

The human body is built of many different parts or organs with different functions, but all the parts work together as one unit. This is also true of the Founder's team of employees. A good example of the Founder's team is found in 1 Corinthians 12:14–20 (NKJV):

For in fact the body is not one member but many. If the foot should say, "Because I am not a hand, I am not of the body." Is it therefore not of the body? If the whole body were an eye, where would be the hearing? If the whole were hearing, where would be the smelling? But now God has set the members, each one of them, in the body just as He pleased. And if they were all one member, where would the body be? But now indeed there are many members, yet one body.

With teamwork, it is important that each member knows the goal of the company and his or her responsibilities in carrying out individual assignments. Both the Founder and the CEO make the goal of the company very clear and how employees are to work together toward achieving that goal. All the operations of the company must work together for the good of the company and its mission—*saving souls*. If employees can't work together at meeting the company's goal, they will not be able to accomplish the Founder's overall purpose.

As with any functional team, each member must sharpen their individual skills and then bring them together with the complementary skills of others to reach a common goal. This implies that each member must pinpoint their dominant skills, assign an individual position to carry out, and then practice their skills together in order to effectively accomplish the team's goal.

Another important quality necessary in developing a good team is accountability. This means that the team members should use insight to help find strengths and weaknesses in one another to collectively become stronger and reach goals. This also means that team members are to help one another in a constructive manner that benefits the whole group. For example, if an employee of the Founder becomes weak to the temptations of life and begins to backslide, the stronger employees should come to the aid of the weaker employee. Romans 15:1 (AMP) maintains that "we who are strong ought to put up with the weaknesses of those who are not strong, and not just please ourselves." This is done by reaching and counseling one another in times of need.

Another example is if an employee becomes physically or mentally handicapped, the stronger employees of the Founder should come to his or her aid to strengthen, pray for, provide for, and nurse the employee back to health. And lastly, if an employee falls to the wiles of Satan and begins to misrepresent the company, then the stronger employees of the Founder should immediately step in to dispose of the false teachings and misrepresentations to bring him or her back in alignment with biblical truths. Never emotionally beat down an employee for making a mistake. Always correct an employee with understanding and love, knowing that you, too, could fall into temptation and you'll need someone to pull you back into the fold.

As with any team, the Founder's team consists of coaches and trainers. These team members usually serve in such positions as chaplains, spiritual teachers, or counselors. Their chief job is to train new employees and help keep the team on track with the goal. Their job is not more important than the jobs of other members of the team. Just as the eyes are not more important than the feet, the service that each member brings to the team is equally important for the team's success as a whole.

*As iron sharpens iron, so a man sharpens the countenance of His friend.*

—Proverbs 27:17 (NKJV)

# Chapter 14

## How to Dress for Success

When people think of dressing, they think of hair, nails, makeup, and all that goes with grooming and clothing the outer appearance. However, it is not so important to look like you've stepped out of *GQ Magazine*, because not all employees of the Founder have expensive or flashy clothing; nor does God make this a requirement to work for His company. What is more important to the Founder is that your heart and mind are clothed with the spirit of righteousness and holiness and that you dress Christlike in your conduct. Yes, you should wash your hair, body, and clothing; but at times, this is not always possible for employees of the Founder who are temporarily on missionary assignments or in a homeless or impoverished condition. It is your *inner* spirit that God is mostly concerned about, and your inner spirit will determine the type of clothing you decide to wear outwardly. We learn this from the Founder's words to His faithful servant Samuel. In 1 Samuel 16:7 (NKJV), it is written:

> But the Lord said to Samuel, "Do not look at his [Saul's] appearance or at his physical stature, because I have refused him. For the Lord

does not see as man sees, for man looks at the outward appearance, but the Lord looks at the heart."

In the scripture above, the Lord rejected Saul as king of Israel because he (Saul) had disobeyed Him. (The inner spirit of Saul was rebellious.) Outwardly, Saul looked the part of a perfect saint, but inwardly, he was far from righteous. Instead, the Lord told Samuel the prophet to go to the house of Jesse, who had eight sons.

Jesse called seven of his sons one by one to meet Samuel, but the Lord told Samuel that none of them were His chosen. So, Jesse then called David, the youngest and smallest son who attended the sheep, into Samuel's presence.

> Then Samuel took the horn of oil and anointed him in the midst of his brothers; and the Spirit of the Lord came upon David from that day forward. So Samuel arose and went to Ramah. (1 Samuel 16:13 NKJV)

You see, David's youth and inexperience didn't disqualify him from being chosen by the Founder to become the next king of Israel. While the outer appearance of his brothers looked the part of a king, the Founder chose David based on how humbly dressed he was *within* his heart.

As employees of the Founder, our dress, in terms of physical appearance and youth, should not take away from who the Founder made us to be inside our heart. We should also be careful not to defile our bodies in any way since this is disrespectful to the Founder and all that He stands for. This includes the Founder's requirement that we are to wear gender-appropriate clothing. Males should dress masculine and conservatively, and females should dress femininely, conservatively, and modestly.

When men and women dress provocatively, extravagantly, and excessively, it gives off a seductive, vain, self-seeking, and self-important attitude. This type of outer appearance can be offensive to others and may cause rivalry among employees of the Founder. We should never strive to outdo one another as employees of the company except in the area of loving one another. Remember that it pleases the Founder when we behave and dress modestly, decently, and appropriately. The Founder makes this clear to us in the Handbook. He instructs and warns both men and women to conduct themselves as follows:

- Women should not wear masculine attire and men should not wear feminine attire.

  *A woman shall not wear anything that pertains to a man, nor shall a man put on a woman's garment, for all who do so are an abomination to the Lord your God. (Deuteronomy 22:5 NKJV)*

- Women, men, or children should not make any cuts of the dead (skulls, bones, etc.) or tattoos on their body.

  *You shall not make any cuttings in your flesh for the dead, nor tattoo any marks on you; I am the Lord.* (Leviticus 19:28 NKJV)

If you placed permanent tattoos on your body prior to coming to know Christ as your personal Savior, you cannot erase what has already been done. The Founder understands your heart and has forgiven you for this action.

- Men are to clothe their minds with understanding and honor toward their wives; otherwise, the Lord will not hear their prayers.

  *Husbands, likewise, dwell with them with understanding, giving honor to the wife, as to the weaker vessel, and as being heirs together of the grace of life, that your prayers may not be hindered.* (1 Peter 3:7 NKJV)

- Women should dress conservatively and behave with wisdom and self-control.

  *Likewise also that women should adorn themselves in respectable apparel, with modesty and self-control, not with braided hair and gold or pearls or expensive attire.* (1 Timothy 2:9 ESV)

- Wives should gently and quietly allow their husbands to lead them, even if the husband is not a Christian yet.

> *Wives, in the same way submit yourselves to your own husbands so that, if any of them do not believe the word, they may be won over without words by the behavior of their wives. Your beauty should not come from outward adornment, such as elaborate hairstyles and the wearing of gold jewelry or fine clothes. Rather, it should be that of your inner self, the unfading beauty of a gentle and quiet Spirit, which is of great worth in God's sight. For this is the way the holy women of the past who put their hope in God used to adorn themselves.* (1 Peter 3:1–6 NIV)

When others look upon you as an employee of the Founder, they should be able to see the purity and respectable character of Christ in your life. Therefore, your conduct and attire must not deflect away from the Founder. Instead, your character and outer appearance should bring those whom you come in contact with closer to righteousness and the enduring life that the Founder wants each of His employees to reflect concerning His ways and His kingdom. In essence, your apparel and grooming should reflect your inner spirit, and your inner spirit should reflect the Founder.

> *Do you not know that your bodies are temples of the Holy Spirit, who is in you, whom you have received from God? You are not your own; you were bought at a price. Therefore honor God with your bodies.*

—1 Corinthians 6:19–20 (NIV)

# Chapter 15

## Employee Evaluation

As an employee of the Founder, He will periodically evaluate your service on earth to determine where you are in your Christlike walk with Him. In many cases, your evaluations come in the form of tests or trials, which will reveal your spiritual strengths and weaknesses. The purpose of these tests and trials, which will come at different stages in your life, is not to expose your weaknesses to others but rather to help you see where you stand in relation to God, the people in your life, and your assignment.

Your spiritual growth and development as a son or daughter of the Founder is necessary to promote and sustain you in your divine purpose. It is through the evaluation process that the Founder will try to keep you on the right track to ensure that you are in His will and that you are fulfilling the great commission of bringing lost souls into His kingdom.

When you receive a passing evaluation from the Founder, your outcomes from it are manifested in the form of additional wisdom, peace of mind, unspeakable joy, meaningful relationships, and physical blessings or favors. Upon every passing test, the Founder elevates you from faith to faith and from glory to glory to glory.

## What to Do When You Fail an Evaluation

Because of the Founder's love and desire for us to reach our maximum potential, He never gives up on us once we are His employees. The only reason that the Founder will let us go is if we decide to permanently terminate our spiritual employment with Him. (More about termination will be discussed in the final chapter of this book.) The Founder will never force His will on anyone. He gives each of us free will to choose His way or our way.

If you fail an evaluation, the *first* thing you should do is remember that it is not the end of your employment with the Founder. The Founder is faithful to fulfill His promise to you: "I will not leave you as orphans, I am coming to you" (John 14:18 NIV).

His promise to you is, however, conditional on your part, which leads to the *second* thing that you should do when you fail an evaluation: seek Him and ask Him—through prayer and petition—to give you the guidance, understanding, and strength you need to follow His ways. When you humbly and sincerely seek Him in prayer, you will receive from Him an understanding of what areas in your life you need to correct to pass future evaluations. The Handbook says, "Ask, and it shall be given you; seek, and ye shall find; knock, and the door shall be opened to you" (Matthew 7:7 KJV).

After the Founder provides you with the answers to correct your spiritual deficiencies, the *third* and final thing that you should do when you fail an evaluation is make a checklist of the issues and place it somewhere you can see it daily. By doing this, you can work on strengthening your weaknesses daily so you may become more effective when dealing with life's problems, as well as help others overcome theirs.

## Tools God Uses to Improve Your Walk with Him

At His discretion, the Founder will use various means to communicate with you to bring you back in right standing with Him. He will communicate with you through the Holy Spirit, through other employees, through opportunities for you to help reconcile broken relationships, through others, through hardships, and through the miracles He performed in your life. Whatever means God will use to improve your walk with Him, choose to embrace it because He truly has your best interest.

Perhaps it's a relationship with which you're having problems and have tried to resolve but the other person continues to show abusive patterns verbally, financially, physically, or sexually—you must assess whether the relationship, be it business or personal, is worth maintaining or not. You have to know, deep within the basement of your spirit, what brings you life and what does not.

> **You have to know, deep within the basement of your spirit, what brings you life and what does not.**

If a person, place, idea, or thing is not producing life and blessings for you—pray and let him, her, or it go. You must press forward toward the mark of the prize for the higher calling on your life through Christ Jesus (Philippians 3:15 KJV). There are hungry, broken people waiting for you to minister to them; you don't have time to waste on people who are hindering you! Get on with the plans that God has for your life so that you'll be blessed to be a blessing to a multitude of people who *want* to be helped.

Another means that the Founder uses to communicate with you and guide you toward corrective action is through chastening. The word *chasten* does not mean to punish; instead, it means to train, instruct, nurture, tutor, or discipline (in order to bring a person back into corrective behavior). It is important to examine yourself to see if you have strayed from the Founder's path in your thoughts, words, and actions. If you have veered off the right path, then the Founder will allow some painful circumstances into your life to cause you to decide to come back to Him. The Handbook informs us of this in Hebrews 12:6 (NKJV): "For whom the Lord loves He chastens, and scourges every son who He receives."

An example of God's chastening can be found in Luke 15:11–32, where Jesus tells the parable of the prodigal son. A wealthy man had two sons. The younger son demanded his share of the inheritance from his father. To avoid a confrontation, the father gave his younger son his inheritance. Then his son left to go to a faraway country. It wasn't long after the boy left that he squandered his inheritance in riotous living. Soon after his money was gone, a famine sprung up in that country, and the boy found himself destitute and starving, so much so that he longed to eat the slop from the pigpen—but not even the pigs would share their food. It was at this critical moment that the boy started thinking sensibly about how good life was when he lived with his father. He knew that he had a choice to either stay in the country where there was a famine and the possibility of starving to death or go back home, where there was unconditional love, acceptance, security, servants—and lots of food!

God will cause a famine or a storm so big to beat up against everything you thought you were big and bad enough to do. Just as God found a way to get the attention of the prodigal son, He will do the same thing to you and me. You might not like how He pulls you out of harm's way, but you will learn to trust and obey Him while being chastised. Case in point, sometimes, God will wreck your life to save or restore it.

> **Sometimes, God will wreck your life to save or restore it.**

Although the boy was embarrassed that he had splurged his inheritance on wild partying, he made a conscious decision to humble himself and return home to serve his father. He remembered that even the servants who lived on his father's estate were well taken care of. So as the boy started walking down the long driveway, the father spotted him afar off. Out of compassion for his son, the father cried and ran to meet him! When he reached his son, the father gave him a big hug and kiss to welcome him back home! With shame in his face, the son looked at the ground, with meekly downcast eyes (like a little child who knows when he has done something wrong), and said to his father, "I have sinned against heaven and against you. I am no longer worthy to be called your son" (Luke 15:21 NIV). But the father dismissed his comments and told his servants:

> Hey, bring the best robe and put it on my son, and put a ring on his finger and sandals on his feet. Also, bring the fattest calf and kill it. We are having a party because my son who was dead [in his sins] is alive again; he was lost and now is found! (Luke 15:22–24 NKJV; emphasis added)

Let this passage on the Founder's chastening of the prodigal son be a reminder of two things: First, a life without God is wasteful, destructive, and meaningless. If you don't remember and defeat your past or present issues, you'll ruin your future. Someone once said that what you do not conquer, you cannot change! Second, God's love for you never fails! The prophet Isaiah makes this declaration in Isaiah 59:1(NIV), "Surely the arm of the Lord is not too short to save [you], nor his ear too dull to hear [when you call for help]." God is your Father, and His arms are always wide open to receive you after you've strayed from His path.

---

**A life without God is wasteful, destructive, and meaningless.**

---

**If you don't remember and defeat your
past or present issues, you'll ruin your future.**

---

Also, keep in mind that the Founder has provided you two simple but major rules to follow. Of course, there are other commandments, as listed in the Handbook, that you should follow as well. But you will greatly improve the outcome of your evaluation when you follow these two rules: Be sure that you are *forgiving* (of yourself and others) and *giving*. When you forgive yourself and others, the Founder will forgive you and release you from the prison of pride, shame, guilt, anger, resentment, and other hurtful emotions that have you constrained, and He will receive you and give you the love that you went all over the world searching for but could not find.

When it comes to giving, give cheerfully and sensibly of your time, talents, spiritual gifts, earnings, and other blessings to help meet the needs of others. In other words, let your light shine by being the hands and feet of Christ. The Founder has promised you that you will receive in exact measure what you give. Both of these rules are documented in the Handbook in Luke 6:37–38 (KJV), in which Jesus informs us,

> Forgive, and you will be forgiven. Give, and it will be given to you; good measure, pressed down, shaken together, and running over shall men give into your bosom. For with the same measure that you use, it will be measured back to you.

## Examining Thyself

This point is where you should do a self-examination to determine where you stand with God's plan for your life and be quick to listen to His voice when change is needed. Some of the questions you should ask yourself are as follows:

- Is my lifestyle pleasing to the Founder, or am I still holding on to sinful habits such as drugs, alcohol, sexual immorality, jealousy, gossip, and lies that are hurting others as well as myself? (Read Proverbs 12:13; Proverbs 28:18; Song of Solomon 8:6; and 1 Thessalonians 4:1–8.)
- Am I hanging out with wise people, or are my friends foolish and unreliable? (Read Proverbs 13:18, 20; Proverbs 14:7–8, 16; Proverbs 15:7; and Proverbs 25:19.)
- Am I teachable, or do I only listen to people who agree with me, even if I am dead wrong? (Read Proverbs 15:4–5, 10, 12, 22, 24; Proverbs 19:20–21; and Psalm 143:10.)
- When people whom I try to help react to me in a negative and dysfunctional manner, do I become emotionally upset and fight along with them and disqualify myself as a true follower of Christ, or do I remain cool, calm, and collected? (Read Proverbs 11:12; Proverbs 12:16; Proverbs 14:29; Proverbs 15:28–29; Proverbs 25:28; and James 1:19.)

- Am I seeking the riches of this world—fame, power, and influence—or am I seeking God's plan for my life? (Read Jeremiah 29:11; Habakkuk 2:2; Proverbs 13:13; Proverbs 15:27; and Proverbs 28:20.)
- Do I treat my spouse, children, extended family, neighbors, strangers, friends, coworkers, and even my enemies with love and kindness? (Read Mark 12:30–31; John 13:34; and Isaiah 58:7–10.)
- Am I passionately pursuing the calling that God has for my life, or am I just drifting along in life because I fear humankind's opinion of me more than God's? In pursuing God, am I forsaking my own ways for His plan? (Read Proverbs 24:27; Proverbs 24:33– 34; Isaiah 49:9; and Isaiah 58:12.)
- Am I preparing my children to become holy, wise, confident, and faithful spouses, parents, coworkers, and spiritual leaders? (Read Psalm 144:12; Proverbs 20:7; Proverbs 22:6, 15; Proverbs 23:15; and Ephesians 6:1.)
- Is there anyone with whom I have fallen out of fellowship with, including God the Father? If so, I accept the invitation for me to come (now) to the throne of grace to ask God to forgive and heal me and the person with whom I have the problem and to bring restoration to the relationship. (Read Ephesians 4:31; Ephesians 4:26; Matthew 18:21–22; Colossians 3:13; Malachi 4:6; Matthew 5:9; and 2 Corinthians 5:2.)
- Now that I have a good understanding about the Founder and the purpose for which He created me, would I take this time to surrender my life to Him? (Read John 3:16 and Romans 10:19.)

In summary, the process of evaluation is necessary in the life of every believer. How you respond to various situations that occur in your life reveals where you are spiritually with God and others and whether nonbelievers will want to seek employment in the company. When you are under satanic attack or facing overwhelming trials, it is important to remind yourself of God's Word. Remember that if you try to fight Satan with his weapons, you will lose every time. But if you fight the good fight of faith by using the Word of God as your weapon of choice, you will win *every* time.

Always evaluate every situation with love, wisdom, understanding, and caution before giving a response. Remember that the Word of God is a two-edged sword that cuts to the core of your bones, exposing and sorting through and judging the very thoughts and purposes of your heart. Remain encouraged, my fellow workers of the Founder, and know that your battles are not fought alone. Divine angels are assisting you; the saints of God are praying on your behalf as well. And finally, in every situation or circumstance remember your A, B, C's—Always Be Christlike!

> *Examine yourselves to see whether you are in the faith; test yourselves. Do you not realize that Christ Jesus is in you—unless, of course, you fail the test?*

—2 Corinthians 13:5 (NIV)

# ❧ **Chapter 16** ❧

## **Promotion**

According to *Merriam-Webster,* there are multiple meanings associated with the word *promotion.* For the purpose of this message, I will use the following meanings: elevation, advancement, or improvement. When you first come on board as an employee of the Founder, you are immediately promoted from your former life. One of the benefits of working for the company is that the promotions are plentiful and employee driven. This means that the higher you go in God, the higher He elevates, advances, and improves your life. Every time you pass a test and trial, He sharpens your vision (to see where He's taking you) and gives you the extraordinary ability to soar above life's problems—like that of an eagle. You don't always realize it, but with every trial that you pass, you're actually in training for the next one. That's why, in the previous chapter, I mentioned that God takes you from faith to faith and from glory to glory to glory—because in your Christian journey, the tests never end. There's always another opportunity for promotion on the way. They just keep coming around until the Founder comes to take you to your eternal home.

> **The higher you go in God, the higher He elevates, advances, and improves your life.**

Imagine working for a company where every employee has a chance to receive multiple promotions based on individual work performance. Unlike earthly employment, positions held, length of time on the job, level of education, managing budgets, and even agreeing to practice corruption are not factors for promotion by the Founder. Instead, you are promoted based on your faithfulness to God, your inward and outward righteous lifestyle, your obedience to the Handbook, and your personal service to the kingdom of God while on earth.

> For promotion cometh neither from the east, nor from the west, nor from the south. But God is the judge: he putteth down one, and setteth up another. (Psalm 75:6–7 KJV)

Contrary to being promoted by the Founder, many employees seek to be promoted by humankind. Proverbs 29:25 (NKJV) states that "the fear of man brings a snare. But he who trusts in the Lord will be exalted." As an employee of the Founder, we should never seek or strive to win the approval of any person because humankind is prone to bribe, manipulate, control, and entrap you for his own personal gain. Our dedication, focus, honor, and loyalty must be to please the Founder and seek His approval if we want to receive His blessings and promotions.

Each time an employee of the Founder is promoted, employees in heaven and on earth literally celebrate. The Founder and His Son are always incredibly pleased any time an employee is promoted. Employee rewards for promotions are long-lasting and priceless in the kingdom of God. Since the Founder owns everything on earth that is wholesome, His priceless rewards should not come as a surprise to you.

The rewards for promotion range from having real, genuine love, peace, joy, wisdom, knowledge, and favor to wealth of honor, health, happiness, and good relationships—the desires of your heart. For some employees, the Founder will even give riches, as was the case with Abraham, Moses, Job, Nehemiah, Solomon, Joseph, and Queen Esther. You might think it's unfair that the Founder chooses the type of blessings He bestows on His employees because some of us receive favor in governing kingdoms while others receive favors in the form of peace, joy, and good health.

But some people are willing to suffer more persecution—personally and *publicly*—for the benefit of all believers than others. There are some Christians who will buckle under the smallest amount of applied pressure, and there are some great faith walkers who will endure much persecution for the survival of all. (For example, the early church was persecuted by the emperors of ancient Rome for the Word's sake in Acts 5:40–42.) Thus, our magnificent Creator God knows the diverse plans that He has for each of our lives as His employees. Therefore, He decides—with His unmistakable discretion—what we need individually for the benefit of all.

**Eight Things You Must Do to Be Promoted by God**

1. Receive God's Word and be born again (John 3:5–6).

2. Be willing to go deeper in His love. Show people the love of God through your actions, not just your words. "He who believes in Him is not condemned; but he who does not believe is condemned already, because he has not believed in the name of the only begotten Son of God" (John 3:18 NKJV).

3. Love Him above all by obeying His commandments. "If you love me, keep my commandments" (John 14:15, 21 KJV).

4. Worship Him in spirit and truth. Worship Him in your heart, not just outwardly. "God is a Spirit: and they that worship Him must worship Him in Spirit and truth" (John 4:24 KJV).

5. Lift his name on high. "Jesus said, 'And if I be lifted up, I'll draw all men unto Me'" (John 12:32 KJV; emphasis added).

6. Do the works of the Founder so that others will believe in Him. "Jesus said, 'If I do not the works of my Father, believe me not. But if I do, though ye believe not Me, believe the works; that ye may know, and believe, that the Father is in Me, and I in Him'" (John 10:37 KJV).

7.  Be willing to go through persecution for Jesus's sake. If you live in opposition to the immoral spirit and deeds of this world, you will be persecuted. "Yea, and all that will live godly in Christ Jesus shall suffer persecution" (2 Timothy 3:12 KJV).

8.  Finally, we must be willing to lay down our own lives for Christ and for our brothers and sisters in Christ. The only way that this can be done by any employee is by sensibly giving your time, possessions, and spiritual gifts to minister to the needs of others (Matthew 14:13).

## Examples of Suffering and the Promotions That Come

The process of promotion can go from simple to complex sufferings, depending on God's purpose for the trial. King Jehoshaphat had to face an army three times the size of his, but because he prayed to God and selected worshippers to go before His throne, God smote his enemies and gave him all their wealth. David had to wander in the desert for several years to avoid death at the anger of King Saul; by doing so, he became the king of Israel. Esther had to risk her life when she became the first woman ever to approach the king's throne; by doing so, she saved the lives of her people and became the queen of Persia. Paul and Silas were thrown into prison at Philippi for preaching the gospel of Christ and for casting an unclean spirit out of a young woman, yet while there, they converted a jailer to accomplish God's will; and God caused the prison doors to open before their eyes. So, we understand that with persecution comes promotion. Some employees receive their promotions on earth while others must wait patiently to receive their rewards when they get to heaven.

The Founder is so lavish with His gifts that in many cases your children and often others around you are blessed also because of *your* promotion! It has been said and proven time and again that one person can change your life for good—forever! Even through the forming of healthy relationships, the employees of the Founder are promoted. Isn't it encouraging *knowing* that you are just *one* person away from receiving a tremendous breakthrough in your life? First Corinthians 15:58 (NIV) states,

> Therefore, my dear brothers, stand firm. Let nothing move you. Always give yourselves fully to the work of the Lord, because you know that your labor in the Lord is not in vain.

When many potential employees are informed of all the wonderful promotions and benefits of working for the Founder's company, in excitement and eagerness, they want to bypass the job requirements and come aboard right away. Many of them miss out because they fail to realize that they must first earnestly accept the terms of agreement of becoming an employee with the Founder's company. They have to count the costs before they commit because to live for the Founder means that one will suffer much affliction. As we have already previously learned, it is impossible to please the Founder without faith. And being faithful to the Founder, even in the time of suffering, is a requirement for promotion.

The Founder's earthly employees have many opportunities to receive numerous promotions as they perform and remain faithful and loyal to the Founder and His principles. When employees are promoted in the Founder's company, it is very contagious. Each time an employee is promoted, the pathways that led to their promotion are called testimonies. The testimonies of promoted employees are wonderful motivators for other employees and are great tools for recruiting new ones. Every good employee is expected to share their personal testimony with others. New employees often use the testimonies of more seasoned employees when they share the company benefits with their family and friends, whom they are trying to recruit into the company.

Being promoted in the Founder's company has no comparison to earthly companies. Earthly companies are often inconsistent and unjust with regard to their promotion policies, if one exists at all. On the contrary, promotions with the Founder's company are just and honest because the Founder is faithful to award His employees who keep His commandments and seek His will. The ultimate promotion that any employee of the Founder can receive is to have his or her name written in the book of life. This is the final promotion that every employee of the Founder wants to receive throughout their physical and spiritual life. This is the utopia for all who love the Founder and everything that He represents. In the Handbook, Jesus, in Luke 10:20 (KJV), tells us,

*"Rejoice because your names are written in heaven."*

# Chapter 17

## Continuing Education

One of the requirements discussed with all new employees during training is the importance of being committed to continuous learning of the all-inclusive Handbook. This commitment to grow in the knowledge of the Founder is expected of every employee who considers him or herself a true disciple of Christ, regardless of the number of years with the company, rank, position, or religious affiliation. It doesn't matter whether you're being taught about Christ in the Baptist, Pentecostal Holiness, United Methodist, or a nondenominational church, as long as you're being taught the Bible in its purest form. Additionally, individual growth within the Founder's company has nothing to do with age.

Spiritual growth is not the same as physical growth. It is a known fact that the younger a person is when he or she truly surrenders their life to Christ, the more loyal and committed they will be when they grow up. Often, many younger employees in the company have more wisdom, love, and compassion for others than the chronologically older employees of the Founder who, at times, become very complacent on their spiritual journey.

The Handbook makes several references to the above point. One of them can be found in Proverbs 22:6 (KJV), which instructs parents to "train up a child in the way that he should go, and when he is old, he will not depart from it." Then in Matthew 11:25 (KJV), Jesus said, "I thank You, Father, Lord of heaven and earth, that You have hidden these things from the wise and prudent and have revealed them to babes."

You may ask yourself the question, How can a child be wiser than an adult? How can a newly converted Christian be wiser than a person who has been saved for ten years? This is possible because a person can be saved for ten years but decide not to "surrender" their life totally to follow Christian principles. Whereas a child who sincerely asks God to take their life and make him or her an instrument to be used for His glory will be granted wisdom, knowledge, and understanding in all things. (Recall this in a previous chapter, James 1:5.) As an employee of the Founder, our quest for wisdom and understanding should be on spiritual concerns to receive the answers we need to take care of our day-to-day natural needs.

When you start your employment with the company, both the Founder and His Son accepts you where you are, but they also expect you to increase your spiritual knowledge and apply it to every aspect of your life. Proverbs 4:7 (KJV) states, "Wisdom is the principal thing; therefore get wisdom: and in all your getting get understanding." Without spiritual wisdom and understanding of the Handbook, your relationships and divine purpose as an employee of the Founder will remain stagnant. Without spiritual growth, your thinking won't change; and without change, your life cannot be elevated (higher).

A secular education is good and quite useful when it is kept in its proper place because everybody needs a trade to contribute to the medical, emotional, financial, educational, recreational, and physical well-being of themselves and others. However, a secular education alone cannot replace nor triumph over spiritual wisdom.

> **Without spiritual growth, your thinking won't change; and without change, your life cannot be elevated (higher).**
>
> ---
>
> **A secular education alone cannot replace nor triumph over spiritual wisdom.**

Earthly education is valuable in that it has the ability to increase your personal income, your communication skills, and your knowledge base to perform the work that you are gifted to do in life. It is also quite useful in passing down knowledge to others who aspire to achieve similar goals, which is a wonderful thing to do because you're making an investment in the lives of our future leaders and homemakers. However, I've often made observations during my fifty-four years on planet earth and have concluded that many highly educated people have used their knowledge and economic status to separate themselves—physically, emotionally, and financially—from the intellectually, developmentally, socially, physically, and economically disadvantaged, which are the very people whom the Founder instructs us all to bless and serve. This selfish and prejudicial attitude—"It's not my concern, problem, or responsibility"— is the major reason why an education alone is insufficient to teach you the "principles" necessary to build a meaningful life, marriage, home, workforce, and government that upholds the fundamental principles of godly living. The Bible is the *only* book that can properly guide the affairs of human beings and their relationships with one another.

On the other hand, when you are spiritually educated, you have true wisdom, which helps you navigate through real-life situations and difficulties that occur both in personal and professional relationships and in the environment in which you live. Spiritual wisdom helps you operate from the mind of the Founder, giving you the insight and foresight that your educational background alone is insufficient to provide. With godly insight and foresight, you have a clear understanding about the world, your purpose, and the people around you, which provides you with the knowledge you need to make wise decisions—with a heart of compassion.

Yes, Jesus taught us to do everything with a heart of compassion and love toward one another. And as God's creation, we need to be reminded that we were awarded our achievements by the Founder. Therefore, no one has the right to brag, boast, or look down on anyone. Because the truth of the matter is this, without the Founder, we can do nothing!

There are many people with bachelor's, master's, and PhD degrees who erroneously think that their education is going to meet all their needs and desires. Some of these same individuals find themselves financially, mentally, physically, relationally, and spiritually bankrupted all because they foolishly said in their heart, "There is no God" (Psalm 14:1 KJV), indicating that God has nothing to do with their intelligence, resources, or educational endeavors. Philippians 2:13 (NKJV) says, "It is God who works in you both to will and to do for His good pleasure." Thus, all great accomplishments come from Him!

Moreover, a doctor, professor, or other professional can be excellent in his field of study but at the same time be impoverished in his or her personal and professional relationships. This is the case because without the Founder living inside the person, there is no fruit of the spirit operating in them that helps them maintain good, healthy relationships with people. Yes, he or she was smart and determined enough to obtain educational degrees yet is functioning on a GED level spiritually and relationally. This is possible because a secular education teaches vocational skills in a particular trade, but it cannot teach a person how to be loving, kind, faithful, patient, gentle, pure-minded, forgiving, self-controlled, or sensitive (toward others).

Many educated people have failed in marriages and relationships all because they believed that they were getting along just fine—*without God*. How can you rid yourself of anger, hatred, jealousy, and a messed-up childhood through pursuing higher education alone? It's not possible because all these aforementioned issues are matters of the heart *(spirit)*, which can only be resolved through a personal relationship with the Founder God. There are plenty of emotionally hurt professionals out there in the world. If you ask my wife, who has worked in the fields of mental-health and education, about the matter, she will tell you that I'm telling you the truth.

You've seen it in the media where a physician, school personnel, politician, professional athlete, or religious leader is charged with domestic violence, sexual misconduct, or murder of a spouse, girlfriend or boyfriend, child, patient, client, coworker, student, or a parishioner. Yes, they are brilliant in their professions, but they lack spiritual knowledge and the fruit of the Spirit to exercise unconditional love, joy, peace, kindness...and self-control.

Some of these people, who are highly regarded in their leadership roles, feel as though the rules that they make their subordinates uphold do *not* necessarily apply to them. That is exactly what Tiger Woods stated during a press release when the media addressed his personal issues of wild partying and adultery, which caused the demise of his marriage and the loss of his sponsorship with major brands. Tiger was operating in the flesh, which never satisfied his deepest longing for God to fill his empty spirit. He was chasing after big titles, big money, fast cars, and fast women—which ended up shipwrecking his life! Proverbs 6:26 (KJV) states,

> For by means of a whorish woman a man is brought to a piece of bread: and the adulteress will hunt for the precious life.

Tiger Woods's example goes to show that without spiritual knowledge and the fruit of the Spirit to guide your life, you will live a bigger-than-life role in society, which will trick you into thinking that you're invincible and above reproach. But reality will soon hit you (like a bullet), and all that you have will be taken from you—your marriage, children, friends, business, dignity, and respect. For this reason, people with these and similar mindsets need continuous education from the Word of God to receive the wisdom, knowledge, and compassion required to correct their immoral thinking and live their lives with integrity. Just as a person needs a vision for their education, he or she needs a vision for their spiritual growth.

---

**Just as a person needs a vision for their education, he or she needs a vision for their spiritual growth.**

---

Just as you cannot master a field of study without first applying yourself to learning, you cannot put into practice what you refuse to learn and apply from the Handbook. The privilege of having a secular education, money, power, and influence over people will never resolve matters of the heart—adultery, partying, alcohol/drug abuse, anger, domestic violence, and so on. These issues of the heart can only be resolved through obtaining a spiritual education by cultivating a real, intimate relationship with the Founder God. In all practicality, a biblical education at home, at church, and in Sunday school is the best environment to properly instill and develop spiritual growth, and it should start as soon as the baby comes out of the mother's womb.

When people think that their high positions, affiliations, and education will clean up their perversion, that's usually when God's correction (through public scrutiny or the legal system) becomes their wake-up call. Nobody is exempt from the consequences and judgment of the Handbook—the Bible. Nobody gets by God! First Timothy 1:9 (KJV) states,

> The law is not made for a righteous man, but for the lawless and disobedient, for the ungodly and for sinners, for unholy and profane, for murderers of fathers and murderers of mothers, for manslayers, for whoremongers, for them that defile themselves with mankind, for manslayers, for liars, for perjured persons, and if there be any other thing that is contrary to sound doctrine.

Higher education cannot make people good, nor can it make them righteous. It can get you a good job, but only a godly character will sustain you in your life's work. Once more, earthly education alone cannot substitute or triumph over spiritual wisdom. No matter how much secular education you acquire, you will always need wisdom from the Handbook to make pure, honorable, and wholesome decisions throughout your life.

---

**Higher education cannot make people good; nor can it make them righteous. It can get you a good job, but only godly character will sustain you in your life's work.**

---

If you desire honor, riches, and an abundant life, you must understand that it begins and ends with spiritual employment. You cannot justifiably have these things without understanding the Founder's will and ways of obtainment. The late Dr. Myles Munroe said, "When purpose is not known, abuse is inevitable." For example, if God gives you a wife and children, but you continue to live as if you are a bachelor, then neglect and abandonment are inevitable. Your actions show that you are not ready for the responsibility that comes with marriage and family. Therefore, what the Founder has put into place for our continuous wellbeing comes with instructions from the Bible. No person can separate themselves from the knowledge of God without suffering severe consequences. As I stated earlier in the book, God would never make Himself unnecessary in the lives of His creation.

> **No person can separate themselves from the knowledge of God without suffering severe consequences.**

The Founder is also consistent and faithful to His Word to us. It is up to each of us as employees of the Founder to be obedient to His instructions, which means that we should strive for spiritual understanding. When we become diligent in studying the Bible and applying His wisdom to our daily lives, then we will enjoy the love, peace, unity, and blessings that come from being in a right relationship with the Founder, others, and ourselves. When we accept the fact that the Founder created us to first get to know Him intimately and follow His Handbook, then we will be able to put all other relationships, occupations, things, and desires into their proper place.

The United Negro College Fund was absolutely right when it coined the slogan, "A mind is a terrible thing to waste." No one should waste the most awesome tool and weapon that the Founder has given to them, but an education without God's Word will lead to a wasted or empty life. With the mind of Christ, you can choose to do what is right in all your relationships—personal and professional—and in every circumstance that you will face in life.

When it comes to learning, spiritual knowledge will help you make wise decisions in every aspect of your life—singlehood, marriage and family, education, work, leisure, and so on. Will you make beneficial choices that lead to an honorable life or corrupt choices that lead to dishonor, shame, and destruction of well-intended relationships? The Founder allows each of us free will. This means, He allows you the power to choose. And there are only two choices in life: a spiritual education (God's way) that lead to abundant life or a secular education (your way) that lead to death, hell, and destruction. It is that simple, but the final choice and decision is yours.

> *As newborn babes, desire the sincere milk of the Word, that ye may grow thereby.*

—1 Peter 2:2 (KJV)

# Chapter 18

## Job Security and Benefits

When you gain an understanding of your purpose on earth as an employee for the Founder, then you also understand and appreciate all the benefits of being in a company that guarantees long-term job security. What this means is this: as an employee hired by the company, you have the most awesome job security of *any* corporation known to humankind! Your job security with the Founder's company is guaranteed as long as you continue to do your job, which is to abide in His love and His Word and maintain a willingness to learn and grow spiritually. Jesus said, "I am the vine, you are the branches. He who abides in Me, and I in him, bears much fruit; for without Me you can do nothing" (John 15:4 NKJV).

This does not mean that you will not make any mistakes along the way, "for all have sinned, and come short of the glory of God" (Romans 3:22 KJV). As mentioned previously, there will be times when your job performance wavers, and you do not pass a test. But when that happens, you can rest assured that unlike earthly employers, God will not terminate your employment with His company nor take away your benefits altogether. He gives all His employees time, sometimes years, to come back in right standing with Him.

Quite the opposite in most earthly companies today, you can come close to putting in thirty to forty years of hard work and dedication to a company, and right before it is time to receive your full retirement benefits, management comes up with some *lame* excuse about budget cuts, and they terminate your employment. No one should ever have to experience such a coldhearted discharge, but this is a corporate practice in the world today. This is the real world, as they call it.

There are so many stories about people who worked many years for a company (putting in long hours and dedicating their lives to it), and when it was time to receive their rewards, the company gave them some cheap watch or ring and sent them on their way. They promised their faithful employees all the "perks" stated in the benefits package, which made them feel secure, but when it was time to deliver on their promise, they reneged.

This is exactly what the *thief* comes to do: to kill, steal, and destroy your life, your hopes, your dreams, and all your benefits from the investments that you made in preparation for your future. Satan comes to employ you for selfish reasons, which will leave you bankrupt emotionally, physically, financially, and spiritually! He comes to take from you, not to give based on a reciprocal relationship. Satan uses shiny, deceitful baits to get people hooked on working for him, but after the shine wears off and the scales have fallen off their eyes, He leaves their lives in shambles—and some actually wake up in hell!

This is not the type of job security that the Boss of heaven and earth has established for you as His employee. He honors all of the hard work and dedication you have given to His company, and He shows great appreciation for your service to His mission of saving souls. He rewards you lavishly for your faithfulness and dedication to His work. He came to give you a prosperous life that is meaningful, purposeful, joyful, and eternal. The moment that you accept Jesus as your personal Lord and Savior is the moment your eternal benefits and job security are certain. The Founder is the ideal Boss of all ages, and He treats His employees very well!

## Married to the Backslider

When you surrendered your life to the Founder, that meant your job security with Him was sealed with this inscription: "The Lord knows those who are His" and "All who belong to the Lord *must* turn away from evil" (2 Timothy 2:19 KJV; emphasis added). The only way you could ever be terminated from the Founder's company is to permanently walk out on Him and not respond to His voice (because you have hardened your heart against Him) when He is telling you "Come back to Me."

Yet even in your backslidden state, God calls you back to Himself so that you can experience everlasting job security in Him. He said in Jeremiah 3:22 (KJV), "Return, ye backsliding children, and I will heal your backsliding."

> And they responded, "Behold, we come unto thee; for thou art the Lord our God."

Unlike an earthly corporation that will permanently terminate you for cheating, lying, or doing some illegal act that causes you to get fired, the Founder will always provide a way for your escape from evil so that you can be restored back into His company. Jesus is the redemption plan to spiritually restore and reconcile you back in good standing.

Maybe it's not a job that you've lost forever but a marriage where someone broke the covenant and it ended in divorce. God said,

> They say, If a man put away his wife, and she go from him, and become another man's, shall he return unto her again? Shall not that land be greatly polluted? But thou hast played the harlot with many lovers; yet return again to me, saith the Lord. (Jeremiah 3:1 KJV)

Although the marriage has been destroyed, God will heal, forgive, and mend you back to health if you repent and come back to Him. You can pray for a wayward spouse who has committed adultery to come back to you, but that does not mean he or she will return. The truth is that every marriage cannot be saved because some married couples are unequally yoked. In order for a marriage to work, both the husband and wife must uphold godly principles. If a spouse makes decisions outside of the Handbook, the marital union won't last. So, if you have suffered a no-fault divorce, God can heal and restore your life once you return to Him—your first love. You see, God, not your spouse, has to be *your* everything!

Maybe you're a child (teen or adult) who is struggling with an identity issue, such as homosexuality; and your family has thrown you away because they are upset, hurt, and embarrassed by your decision to turn away from godly teaching. But God is gently saying to you, son or daughter, if you will turn from your sins and return to Him, "I will restore the hearts of the fathers to their children and the hearts of the children to their fathers, so that I will not come and smite the land with a curse" (Malachi 4:6 KJV).

Perhaps you're in jail or prison right now for doing some criminal act, and your friends and family have terminated their relationship with you. Dear friend, God is saying to you, "The man of too many friends will be broken in pieces and come to ruin, but there is a friend who sticks closer than a brother" (Proverbs 18:24 AMP).

Maybe you're a businessman or businesswoman, and your partners allowed you to borrow money from the bank to get the company back in the black, but now they all have left you with the personal responsibility of paying it all back. God is saying to you,

> I will go before thee, and make the crooked places straight: I will break in pieces the gates of brass, and cut in sunder the bars of iron: And I will give thee the treasures of darkness, and hidden riches of secret places, that thou mayest know that, I the Lord, which call thee by thy name, am the God of Israel. (Isaiah 45:2–3 KJV)

Regardless of what your situation is—no matter who has forsaken, rejected, or terminated you from their life—the Founder has a secured position for you waiting in His company to be filled forever! It is not based on your past evaluations, accomplishments, or who you know, but it is based on you surrendering your life to Him and trusting His guidance. No matter who left or rejected you, God's love for you will never fail!

## Benefits

We all know that company benefits are what usually attract us to our earthly employment. Within earthly employment, we usually seek as a part of our benefits medical, dental, and life insurance; 401(k) or other savings plans; paid time off from work for sicknesses and for leisure; scheduled raises; bonuses; and promotional opportunities. Many of us would say that we have a "good job" if we find employment with these benefits. If you are fortunate enough to have all these wonderful benefits in your earthly employment or business, know that your earthly employment or business ownership is *secondary* to your employment with the Founder.

Many of the benefits of working for the Founder have been previously mentioned. The ultimate benefit of working for the Founder is that you will receive eternal job security regardless of who may terminate you from their lives here on earth. All of His employees also receive open two-way communication with Him and His Son. As His employee, you also receive true freedom from condemnation and triumph over life's challenges. Spiritual blessings are in abundance for employees of the Founder! Each obedient employee also enjoys a life that is righteous, holy, and pleasing to the Founder. Employees of the company enjoy the knowledge of their true purpose on earth—to serve the Founder and use the talents and gifts that He has provided them in service of others.

Establishing wonderful camaraderie with other employees of the company is an added benefit as well. For every employee of the Founder can both give and receive encouragement that will create a special bond with one another and maintain the company's morale.

The final but especially important benefit of every employee is being filled with the Holy Spirit. This means that the Founder has provided each employee with a *personal assistant* directly from heaven. As mentioned previously, the Holy Spirit is your helper, counselor, and comforter. He lives within you to keep constant watch over you and guide you in all matters. God uses the Holy Spirit to shield you from getting into things that He knows will end up hurting and deterring you from your eternal benefits and job security. Consider the Holy Spirit as your personal GPS to the Founder. What a wonderful benefit it is to be an established employee of the Founder!

> *Now He who establishes us with you in Christ and has anointed us is God, who also has sealed us and given us the Spirit in our hearts as a guarantee.*

—2 Corinthians 1:21–22 (NKJV)

# Chapter 19

## Retirement

While earthly employees are working on their earthly jobs, they dream of the day when they can retire and spend the last phase of their lives on vacation. Besides, everybody wants the security, tranquility, and comfort of living an independent and carefree life in their elderly years, right? As that time approaches, most seniors hold the idea: "I've worked extremely hard during my youthful days. Now it's time to really enjoy life and do some of the things that I never got the chance to do." As a result, they might start checking out their corporate or government pension programs and looking to downsize, planning to move either to the beach or to the mountains. It does sound like a good way for people to retire and live out the final days, months, or years of their lives. But what people should have been doing all along is enjoying life, family, work, and leisure by allowing Christ to lead every aspect of their lives. Because the real truth of the matter is that an earthly retirement plan is not guaranteed. Nor is tomorrow promised to any of us.

It has been statistically documented that most people do not live much longer past the traditional retirement age, and tens of millions of elderly Americans will not have any money upon retirement. There will not be a social security system in place because the United States government—who was supposed to have $2.5 trillion dollars in the Social Security Trust Fund for the baby boomers—has (in the past thirty years) "borrowed" all the money to pay off debt (*The American Dream 2012*). In March 2020, the Coronavirus pandemic hit globally and shut down our churches, businesses, and schools. The world, as we once knew it, changed forever. Life will never be the same again! Thankfully, the American government paid out trillions of dollars to help its citizens survive this crisis. Nevertheless, these statistics are troubling, but if you are a child of the Boss, you need not be afraid of your future. Throughout the Bible, the Founder warns us of how hard times will be in the last days, and yes, we are living in the last days. God warns us that in the last days perilous times shall come, and people will be lovers of themselves and money, proud, abusive, disobedient to their parents, ungrateful, without self-control, brutal, and lovers of pleasure more than lovers of Him (read 2 Timothy 3:2–5).

So, you cannot put your trust in the stock market, government programs, your 401(k), or anyone or anything that looks promising. This world system is failing every single day. Many retirees have lost everything that were promised them by their earthly bosses, the government, their investment bankers, and so on. The leaders of this world have robbed many people blind by committing white collar crimes.

As an employee of the Founder, you need to *first* understand that this world is *not* your home. And *second*, you need to understand that the highest and ultimate retirement that you will positively receive is your reward for being a resident in heaven. This is the most important part of your employment in the Founder's company—the inheritance of His eternal retirement plan!

When an employee retires from the Founder's company (on earth), it is truly a time for victorious celebration because they have passed on from this earthly life and entered heaven! This eternal retirement plan is in addition to all the benefits that employees of the Founder enjoy *throughout* their lives here on earth. Therefore, your continuous obedience to and labor for God is not in vain. The Founder reminds us of this in Hebrews 6:10 (KJV):

> For God is not unrighteous to forget your work, and the labor of love which you showed toward His name, in that you served the saints, and still do serve them.

As mentioned previously, there are only two choices in life to follow—the Founder's plan and will or Satan's (your own) plan. Satan's plan is hidden behind humankind's broken promise of a loaded retirement that is actually bankrupt. Wouldn't you rather have the real McCoy of a retirement plan? Only the Founder can offer you that!

---

**Satan's plan is hidden behind humankind's broken promise of a loaded retirement that is actually bankrupt.**

---

The Handbook never promises us that the Founder's eternal retirement plan is easy to achieve. Any employee who desires to receive the highest honor of having their name added to the book of life and receive the Founder's retirement plan must endure hardship (like a good soldier) until the end. To reach this honor, you must apply much faith in the Founder's Word and exercise spiritual discipline to follow biblical instructions throughout your life. For all who fear God and stand up for Him in the midst of persecution and perilous times will receive the inheritance of His eternal retirement plan—heaven! God *will* make good on His promises to you!

> *The Lord knows the days of the upright, and their inheritance shall be forever.*

—Psalm 37:18 (KJV)

# Chapter 20

## Termination

As with earthly employment, to be terminated from the Founder's company is never a good experience. But because of humankind's sinful nature to lie, hate, steal, kill, and show preferential treatment, earthly terminations or firings are not always fair or justified. However, to be terminated from the Founder's company is the ultimate of firings, and the cause is *always* justified; His judgments are true and righteous. And this termination is irreversible and eternal! Those who reject the Founder, His Son, and the Holy Spirit will live in torment forever in spiritual death and hell and will be cast into the lake of fire. No one will be excused for *not* knowing God, for God will provide everyone an opportunity to receive His Word (the Handbook) and obey His commandments. According to Romans 1:20–21 (KJV), the Handbook will be preached throughout the earth to all men (emphasis added):

> For the invisible things of Him from the creation of the world [that includes everybody and everything] are clearly seen, being understood by the things that are made, even His eternal power and Godhead: so

that they are without excuse. Because that, when they knew God, they glorified Him not as God, neither were thankful; but became vain in their imaginations, and their foolish heart was darkened.

You see, the invisible things or mysteries of God are revealed through the Handbook and through God's servants for all creation to clearly hear, know, and understand His eternal power and Godhead (Father, Son, and Holy Spirit). Therefore, when Jesus comes back to judge humankind for their deeds, all (small and great) will stand before Him to give an account according to what is written in the judgment books—the book of life and other books.

Whoever is not written in the book of life will be cast into the lake of fire, where Satan, the beast, and all the false prophets will be. "And whoever was not written in the book of life will be cast into the lake of fire" (Revelation 20:15 KJV). To be tossed into hell is the ultimate of firings! For those who deliberately disobey God and cause His children, the employees of the Founder, to be misled into sin, hell is their eternal residence, and destruction is the final condition of their soul.

## Two Deaths: Physical and Spiritual

Anyone who says, "We only live once" is a liar, because there are two deaths! According to Revelation 20:6, the first death is when everyone dies a physical death. The second death is when everyone takes on their spiritual body, which will live forever, in either heaven or hell. (Remember Christ died a physical death, but He rose again in His spiritual or glorified body.) Those who are in Christ in the first resurrection will not have to worry about the second death because they will be found holy, blameless, and undefiled before Christ. Therefore, they will reign with Him for a thousand years. And after the thousand years are complete, Satan will be loosed from the bottomless pit for a short time to deceive and cause those who follow him to deceive others. In spite of this, he will be unable to deceive the employees of God because the Founder will send fire down from heaven (the Word of

God) and devour Satan and his followers. In Revelation 20:7–9 (KJV), John of Patmos wrote:

> And when the thousand years are expired, Satan shall be loosed out of his prison, and shall go out to deceive the nations which are in the four quarters of the earth, Gog and Magog, to gather them together to battle: the number of whom is as the sand of the sea. And they [Satan and his followers] went up on the breadth of the earth, and compassed the camp of the Saints [Christians] about, and the beloved city [Jerusalem]: and fire came down from God out of heaven, and devoured them.

Now it is evident here in these scriptural passages that the Founder will save His employees from being deceived and devoured by Satan, and He will destroy Satan and his followers by casting them into the lake of fire and brimstone to be tormented forever. It is written, "And the devil that deceived them was cast into the lake of fire and brimstone, where the beast and the false prophet are, and shall be tormented day and night forever and ever" (Revelation 20:10 KJV).

Before the judgment of the earth, the angels shall come forth and sever the wicked from the just (Matthew 13:40). When Satan is thrown into the lake of fire, the employees of the Founder who are still alive in their earthly bodies and the dead in Christ will rise and be changed (from their mortal bodies) into their immortal or glorified bodies to live forever with Christ. Only the righteous will enter the gates of heaven and remain with the Founder and His Son, Jesus, forever. The nonemployees of the Founder who rejected Christ will be changed from their mortal bodies into their immortal bodies also, but they will *not* enter the gates of heaven. They will be separated eternally from Christ and put into a furnace of fire; there will be wailing and gnashing of teeth (read Matthew 13:42).

Without receiving Christ, you have no hope for eternal life in heaven (read Revelation 20:11). And, frankly speaking, nobody will get by the judgment of Christ!

## Final Decision: Only One Choice

With this knowledge, you might be thinking, *Why should I become an employee of the Founder and run the risk of being terminated?* The answer is simple: If you decide to continue to straddle the fence, then you will be terminated from the earthly blessings that God promised to bestow on your life and be terminated from heaven. What the Founder offers to every living soul is His plan of salvation, which is the path to abundant life on earth and eternal life in heaven! Second Peter 3:9 (NIV) states (emphasis added),

> The Lord is not slow in keeping His promise, as some understand slowness. He is patient with you, *not wanting anyone to perish*, but everyone to come to repentance.

Either you accept His plan of salvation and become one of His employees or you reject it and forfeit your eternal home with the Founder. This means that you cannot remain in the middle with your decision, for Christ said in Revelation 3:15–16 (KJV),

> I know thy works, that thou art neither cold nor hot: I would thou wert cold or hot. So then because thou art lukewarm, and neither cold nor hot, I will spue thee out of my mouth. Because thou sayest, I am rich, and increased with goods, and have need of nothing; and knoweth not that thou art wrecked, and miserable, and Spiritually poor, blind and naked.

Remember that all your decisions in life are based on two choices: righteousness or evil (unrighteousness). Will you choose the Founder or the impostor? There is no middle ground. Hence, you cannot be partially good and partially evil at the same time. The Founder makes this very clear throughout the Bible.

In choosing the Founder, you are choosing His ways and His instructions for your life. The Handbook has wholesome answers for any situation that you will ever face throughout your lifetime. All you have to do is seek Him and His Word; He will never lead you astray.

The Handbook is full of real-life stories of employees who were terminated from the Founder's company. The first employee to be terminated from heaven was Satan (a.k.a., Lucifer, the devil). As the Handbook informs us, Satan was originally an angel who was created by the Founder for the purpose of leading praise and worship in heaven. But pride, jealousy, and greed for power caused him to try to overthrow the plans of the Founder and make himself equal to Him.

The fact that Satan became rebellious and evil in his ways may have you questioning, why did God create him in the first place? The answer is this: God created the angels and humankind as perfect beings with free will. Satan decided to go against the Founder, and he and a third of the angels (who followed him) were ultimately terminated as a result of disobedience. This is mentioned in the Handbook in Ezekiel 28:15–16 (NKJV) when the Founder spoke to Ezekiel concerning Satan:

> You were perfect in your ways from the day you were created, Till iniquity was found in you. By the abundance of your trading, you became filled with violence within, and you sinned; Therefore, I cast you as a profane thing out of the mountain of God; And, I destroyed you, O covering cherub, from the midst of the fiery stones.

Now that you understand why Satan, an angel, was terminated by the Founder, you may still be unclear why the Founder would terminate a man or a woman. As stated previously, a man or a woman runs the risk of being terminated from the Founder when either consistently rejects the Founder's Word, His Son, His ways, or His will and plans. This rejection (which ends in termination by the Founder) is not based on one's ignorance or one's naivety about the Founder. The Handbook makes it clear that the Founder terminates men and women who have *full* knowledge of Him but continue to reject Him.

To be associated with others who have rejected the Founder is dangerous for you. The Handbook informs us that the Founder's employees are not to love or associate with those who have rejected the Founder because they love the world—the world hates God. Again, this is not to be confused with an employee's commission by the Founder to minister to and reach out to those who have not been fully informed about the Founder. We should always reach out in love to those who have not yet heard or accepted the Son of the Founder to shed light upon the darkness that is in their lives. However, it is not our right to force them to accept God and His Son. It is up to them to decide whom they will serve.

Also, know that continual rejection of the Founder not only keeps a person out of heaven but also has earthly consequences. No one will escape the consequences of their sins even if they have repented of them. The Handbook contains numerous stories of men and women who repented of their sins, but the consequences that they had to live with caused them and others pain. The Founder's judgments are always just, and He does chasten the ones whom He loves. However, it is the continual rejection after *knowing* the truth about the Founder that causes men and women to be eternally terminated and separated from Him.

You see, a person can have full knowledge of the Founder and still reject Him because they are wrapped up in themselves and the creation (which they can physically see with their carnal eyes) rather than the Creator Himself. When a person is consumed with worldliness, they willingly choose the lies of Satan over the truth of the Founder, and they serve the creation more than the Creator (read Romans 1:25). One of the scriptures in the Handbook concerning this issue of choice is found in 1 John 2:15–17 (NKJV):

> Do not love the world or the things in the world. If anyone loves the world, the love of the Father is not in Him. For all that is in the world—the lust of the flesh, the lust of the eyes, and the pride of life—is not of the Father but is of the world. And the world is passing away, and the lust of it; but he who does the will of God abides forever.

Having read this book, you now have the full knowledge of the Founder's plan and purpose, which is to reclaim His children. Now that you have been fully informed of His will for your life, you must make God the Father and Jesus the Son your Lord and Savior. He has completely given you the gift of free will to choose whom you will serve from this day forth. I encourage you not to wait another day to decide to choose God, for tomorrow is not promised to you. The only day that you have is this moment right now. Please understand that a nonresponse is a decision to remain where you are presently—unsaved and bound for eternal hell.

To choose the Father, the Creator of heaven and earth, you must verbally and earnestly accept His Son, Jesus, and acknowledge that He died for you. Then, ask the Father to enter your heart through the Holy Spirit where He will then reside in you. That is the first step in choosing the Father. The Father's support system, beginning with the Holy Spirit, is available to you immediately once you have chosen Him. Just ask Him to come to you, teach you all things, and comfort you during the trials of your life.

There is no gift that can ever be given to you or me to replace or triumph over *Jesus*. If you seek God first, you will receive a crown in heaven! But if you seek Him last, you will be thrown into the lake of fire where there is *everlasting* torment. Always remember, a righteous mind is never forsaken, and a righteous person is never forgotten.

> *And I saw the dead, small and great, stand before God; and the books were opened: and another book was opened, which is the book of life: and the dead were judged out of those things which were written in the books, according to their works....And whosoever was not found written in the book of life was cast into the lake of fire.*

—Revelation 20:12, 15 (KJV)

---

**A righteous mind is never forsaken, and a righteous person is never forgotten.**

---

# Afterword

## The Invitation

If you have already made Jesus, the CEO, your Lord and Savior prior to reading this book, then I hope that after reading this book, your faith has been recharged, your love walk has increased, and a radical change has taken place in the way that you see your life and purpose as an employee of the Founder.

If, after reading this book, you have decided to accept or rededicate your life to Jesus as your personal Lord and Savior, then the author of this book and his coworkers in Christ welcome you as an employee in the company—the Kingdom that shall never end! I would like for you to repeat after me:

> Father God, I admit that I am a sinner, only saved by Your grace. I know that Jesus willingly laid down His life to heal, deliver, and redeem me from my sins and to show me the path to righteousness. So right now, I sincerely ask You to forgive me for rejecting You and going my own way. Please come into my heart (mind) and govern my life forever. Lord, I receive Your precious gift, the Holy Spirit, to seal my life to You and to comfort me when I'm hurting, strengthen me when I'm weak, and guide me along life's journey. Thank You, Abba

Father, for giving me an abundant life through Yahshua the Christ! I love and trust You!

Amen.

You are now on your way to receiving the faith, confidence, spiritual education, promotions, job security, and *eternal* retirement plan that the Father has promised you! *You* are now one of *His*! Go forth, make disciples, and spread the message that heaven is highering!

# About the Author

Weldon R. Johnson is a highly gifted, anointed, and well-informed *outreac*h minister, life coach, Christian author, and visionary. He was the founder and pastor of Resurrection Outreach Ministries of Oklahoma City, Oklahoma, where he and his wife launched Seeds for Souls Mission Outreach to teach, feed, comfort, and befriend lonely and hurting souls in nursing homes, prisons, juvenile detention centers, and the streets. In collaboration with his wife, Pastor Johnson was also the co-founder of AIM Youth 4 Christ, a nonprofit organization that provided mentoring, tutoring, and biblical counseling to at-risk youth in the Oklahoma City metropolitan area.

Because of all the problems around us today, such as the following: COVID-19 pandemic; school, church, and job closings; unemployment being at an all-time high; trust and honesty becoming virtues of the past; and false prophets infiltrating and governing the new-and-improved Babylon, Yahweh (God) has chosen His faithful servant, Pastor Johnson, to boldly speak His Word as a means of instructing, correcting, motivating, and winning people to Christ. As an act of *love* for all humankind, it is Pastor Johnson's earnest desire that everyone will come to know that heaven is highering so that no one will be lost but rather have the opportunity to gain spiritual employment on earth as it is eternally in heaven!

Pastor Johnson is happily married to Victoria, a dynamic life coach, Christian educator, worship singer, and breast cancer survivor! They have two children, Jordan and Sara, and a grandson named Julian.

# Contact Information

Weldon is available for book signings, seminars, conferences, interviews, and various speaking engagements throughout the United States and abroad.

You may contact weldon24heavenishighering@gmail.com to schedule an appointment with him.

Thank you in advance for your support of our ministry!

Printed in the United States
by Baker & Taylor Publisher Services